Large Group Guidance Activities:

A K-12 Sourcebook

by

Joe Wittmer, Ph.D.

and

Diane W. Thompson, M.Ed.

Interpersonal Communication and Cooperation
Cross-Cultural Awareness and Communication
Academic Survival Skills
Decision Making
Personal Assessment and Awareness
Responsible Behavior

Copyright 1995
Joe Wittmer

Library of Congress Catalog Card No. 95-60208

ISBN 0-932796-70-2

Printing (Last Digit)

10   9   8   7   6   5   4   3

Publisher—

Educational Media Corporation®

PO Box 21311

Minneapolis, MN 55421-0311

(612) 781-0088

Production Editor—

Don L. Sorenson

Graphic Design—

Earl Sorenson

Dedication

**This book is dedicated to
two very important people in our lives;
our spouses, Sue and Buddy.**

The Authors

Joe Wittmer, Ph.D. is Chair and Distinguished Service Professor of Counselor Education at the University of Florida, Gainesville, and serves as Coordinator of the School Counselor preparation program. He has been a teacher and a school counselor, and serves as a consultant to school systems desiring to implement developmental school counseling programs.

Dr. Wittmer has written more than 75 professional journal articles and has authored or co-authored ten books. His books include: *The Teacher as Facilitator* (Co-author, 1989); *Valuing Diversity and Similarity: Bridging the Gap Through Interpersonal Skills* (1992); and *Managing Your School Counseling Program* (1993).

Diane W. Thompson, M.Ed. is a full-time counselor at Melrose Elementary School, Melrose, Florida and is a candidate for the Specialist of Education Degree in School Counseling at the University of Florida, Gainesville. Ms. Thompson was a middle school teacher for five years and has been a school counselor eight years. She has been awarded a Delta Theta Tau Fellowship to study toward a Ph.D in School Counseling.

The objectives of this book are to provide the reader an overview and a general understanding of large group developmental guidance and to provide structured K-12 classroom activities to use with students in large group settings. Teachers assigned as "advisors" in *Teachers as Advisors Programs (TAP)* will find the book especially helpful.

In the introductions to each of the six sections we have briefly presented the background and the theme of that particular section. The intended grade levels listed for each activity are based on our experiences with such activities. *Thus, it is our belief that each activity can be adapted to most any grade level by a creative counselor or teacher. Additionally, many of these activities can easily be applied and used in small group counseling situations.*

Through the 1960s, 1970s, and into the 1980s many group activities and techniques were developed to help people "encounter" themselves and others, to increase personal awareness, and to improve communication skills. Early on, personal growth centers became refuges for those who were seeking personal discovery and a better understanding of interpersonal relationships. It was not long before it was realized that everyone could benefit from self-development and that it was a good idea to begin early when young people are in school.

Many of the same activities and techniques that were considered successful, or at least interesting, were proposed for use in classrooms. They hoped that playing some "group games" would compensate for the missing affective component in the classroom. However, these educators quickly learned that the exercises in and of themselves were limited. Many also lacked knowledge, skill, and experience in how to apply these procedures in schools. It became apparent that few teachers, and not all counselors, were effective large group leaders. They needed to know more about how to build group cohesiveness, a climate for more participation and to value personalizing a learning experience. Fortunately, many school counselors and teachers now possess these skills.

For better or worse, there have been many attempts to introduce affective education programs and activities into the school to teach "the whole child." School boards have approved affective curricula with stated goals lined up along side academic goals. In the past these were considered parallel outcomes, and some said that affective education was the predecessor of academic knowledge. Others have claimed that it was best viewed as an integrated part of all learning, not only a humanizing of education, but a personalized and relevant approach. Regardless, affective education is definitely more than a few affective group activities.

The large group guidance activities found in this book are simply a means to an end. The end, in this case, is an increased opportunity for further self-exploration, understanding, and personal involvement. Group procedures and techniques are only a vehicle, and without an effective "driver" they will not help students reach their destinations. School counselors and others who know how to respond to students in facilitative ways tend to be most successful when using such activities.

Educational Media Corporation®, Box 21311, Minneapolis, MN 55421-0311

That is, they do not rely entirely on the structure of the group experience. They realize that it is not the "activities" in and of themselves that are important, it's how the "user," the educator, responds to the student data generated by such activities.

Those counselors, and others who do not understand the value of facilitatively responding to students, frequently report that their group activities fail and they erroneously conclude the procedures have no relevancy. It is especially essential for school counselors to understand how facilitative skills and the activities interrelate. When these are combined and integrated into the regular classroom curriculum, or through a specific large group guidance component, personal and academic growth are facilitated. Thus, counselors are urged to use their unique facilitative "counseling" skills, both individual and group skills, when using these activities.

This book introduces several large group guidance activities and is divided into the following six sections:

I.   Interpersonal Communication and Cooperation

II.   Cross-Cultural Awareness and Communication

III. Academic Survival Skills

IV.   Decision Making

V.   Personal Assessment and Awareness

VI.   Responsible Behavior.

Counselors, working cooperatively with teachers, may want to use these activities as an integrated part of the regular school curriculum or in their TAP program. Or, they may prefer to set aside a certain time when the activities will be used as part of the school's guidance program. On the other hand, some may want to use them as resource units to be drawn upon when a particular situation arises within their school which needs more personal exploration and insight.

Many of these activities are like the folk music of human relations training and the origins of many are difficult, if not impossible, to trace. We are sorry if credit has not been appropriately given where due and we will make every effort to correct any omissions in subsequent revisions. It was not our intent to list all the available group activities and procedures that lend themselves to facilitating personal growth and affective learning in the classroom. However, we have several structured, basic guidance activities to illustrate the six areas noted above.

Several contributors wrote activities specifically for this book. This is to acknowledge our heartfelt thanks to each such contributor and to others whose activities we adapted for use.

Joe Wittmer

Diane W. Thompson

April, 1995

Table of Contents

References and Acknowledgments

Thanks to each of the writers who contributed to this book. A special thanks to Donna Johnson for all her typing and dedicated work making this book possible. Appreciation is also extended to Sharon Lake for her assistance in typing the manuscript.

Acknowledgment and appreciation is extended to the following for permission to reprint/adapt from their publications:

1. *Developmental Guidance for School Success Skills: A Comparison of Modeling and Coaching* by Marjorie Cuthbert, Doctoral Dissertation, University of Florida, 1987.

2. *F.A.M.E. (Finding Acceptance in the Middle School Environment)*; The Alachua County School Board, Gainesville, Florida.

3. *I.M.P.A.C.T. ((Interdisciplinary Middle School Program for Advisement/ Counseling/Teaming)*; Orange County Public Schools, Orlando, Florida.

4. *Sexual Harassment and Teens* by Susan Strauss with Pamela Espeland. Free Spirit Publishing, Inc., Minneapolis, Minnesota, 1992.

5. *The Teacher as Facilitator* by Joe Wittmer and Robert D. Myrick. Educational Media Corporation, Minneapolis, Minnesota, 1989.

6. *Valuing Diversity and Similarity: Bridging the Gap Through Interpersonal Skills* edited by Joe Wittmer. Educational Media Corporation, Minneapolis, Minnesota, 1992.

Every effort has been made to give proper acknowledgment to all those who have contributed to this book. Any omissions or errors are regretted and, upon notification, will be corrected in subsequent editions.

Joe Wittmer, Ph.D. and Diane W. Thompson, M.Ed.

Large Group Guidance: An Introduction*

Large group guidance is the systematic delivery of age-appropriate, preventative (developmental) guidance concepts and units to large groups of students, usually in a school classroom setting. As with the management of any classroom-size group around a chosen curriculum or a specific program, selected techniques to enhance the delivery are used to help facilitate discussion, processing, and learning.

Large group guidance sessions provide unlimited opportunities for counselors to get to know significant numbers of students at any age or grade level. In addition, it permits counselors to capitalize on the energy the larger group naturally provides by the diversities of the backgrounds and experiences of the group members. Even though all students may not get a chance to present their own thoughts or feelings about a topic each session, they are exposed to a broad array of others' ideas. The large grouping allows those students who are shy and have not yet developed the skills to speak out in the groups to be exposed to their peers' perceptions on various topics. The large group format also allows those who choose not to participate to be in a group setting which, by its design, allows them to be a part of a peer group without the pressure of having to perform.

From leading the large group, the counselor learns which students have difficulties managing their behavior in large group settings. These students can later be considered for inclusion in small groups or individual counseling to address specific behavioral needs where skills can be introduced and practiced. When the students have practiced chosen skills in the smaller group, the real test comes when they return to the large group setting. Often this test comes for the regular classroom teachers, but it is particularly effective if the counselor can monitor the targeted behaviors in the classroom when delivering large group guidance lessons.

Not only do large groupings of students for guidance units allow the counselors to know many students, this delivery system also allows counselors to be seen as "teachers of curriculum" by their colleagues. It helps dispel the misconception that counselors are teachers who no longer can or want to manage large groups of students. It helps also dispel the misconceptions that counselors, particularly at the high school level, do mostly paperwork and do not interact with students. When the counselor demonstrates effective techniques for classroom management during the large group guidance sessions, the counselor will be seen as a potential consultant.

It is beneficial for classroom teachers to remain in the room when units are being delivered so they can do follow-up exercises. It is an optimum time for the counselor to utilize skills and model techniques that work effectively with all kinds of student populations. Because of this exposure, it becomes a major responsibility of counselors to develop sound units which are age-appropriate and deliver them professionally. Counselors in these settings are powerful agents of change for both teachers and students.

*Adapted from Cuthbert, M. (1987). *Developmental guidance for school success skills: A comparison of modeling and coaching.* Doctoral Dissertation, University of Florida.

Effectiveness of Large Group Guidance Lessons

Large group guidance units are an accepted delivery model and have been found to be effective and efficient vehicles to use with students of all ages. Many studies involving different age levels and varied content have shown positive changes in outcome variables as evaluated by both students and teachers. There are many methods and instruments available to evaluate units.

As can be seen by the areas presented in this handbook, many different topics can be delivered to large groups. School counselors at all levels can create (or locate) units to meet objectives which often include ideas of understanding self and others, getting along with peers, dealing with peer pressure, accepting limitations, capitalizing on strengths, recognizing differences, using conflict resolution techniques, developing cultural awareness, learning communication and interpersonal skills, and exploring careers. Any of the topics could be easily put into systematic units for delivery, keeping in mind the age to which they would be delivered so appropriate developmental concepts can be included and age appropriate activities chosen.

This book contains activities for large group guidance designed for high school, middle school, and elementary school students. High school counselors meet success with large group guidance units dealing with registration procedures and issues that arise when students are transitioning from grade level to grade level. The middle school counselors also deliver large group guidance lessons to their eighth graders as they move from middle school to high school. They address some specific procedures, but also attend to all the social and emotional changes that accompany these level changes. Addressing similar developmental changes and concerns, developmentally oriented elementary counselors deliver large group units to fifth graders as part of the orientation process for middle school.

High school counselors also meet with large groups of students to discuss results from interest surveys and career counseling instruments. They group college bound students to counsel with them about writing resumes and application essays, and to make them aware of general ways to look at colleges to meet personal needs and financial realities.

Middle school counselors help large groups work on career plans that cut across all the high school years which might include college, vocational opportunities, or general areas of study. Along this same topic, elementary counselors deliver units on career awareness which serve as the starting points for the other levels to build upon. As can be observed from the flow of an effective K-12 career education program, counselors often deal with the same topic at different levels and adjust the information given and its processing to the developmental level of the students.

Elementary school counselors deliver classroom guidance lessons on most of the topics listed above. Most local, district, or county guidance programs list goals and objectives for the different grade levels. Elementary counselors can best realize these objectives through 20- to 30-minute sessions in individual classroom settings, usually conducted once or twice a week for a total of four to six sessions depending on the content of the unit being delivered.

Implementing the Guidance Unit

When and how to deliver developmental guidance units are important topics. We suggest that counselors work closely with a guidance committee in their school to plan out a yearly calendar including time to work with large groups of students. In crowded curricula, it is very important for counselors to be included in master planning, so that time to work with students is given with everyone's knowledge of how guidance services enhance the school environment for students. Elementary counselors plan with the guidance committee or grade level chairpersons to schedule blocks of time which allow for delivery of classroom guidance units of about 30 minutes for six sessions in every classroom. Of course, with counselor to pupil ratios often exceeding 1:600, it becomes difficult to meet this standard and sessions are cut down in number, or several classes are grouped together for a very large group delivery. This latter method works well for some topics, but can become impersonal if used too much for topics that demand more individualized discussions.

Middle and high school counselors often arrange to deliver career planning or college planning guidance units during chosen classes (e.g., all English classes or all math classes). When they are able to do this, they know they have reached the majority of their students. Many middle and high schools have designated a block of time at the beginning of each day where teachers give out necessary information about scheduling and planning. They also help deliver chosen guidance objectives of the developmental plan. These blocks of time where teachers are delivering guidance components are often referred to as "Teacher Advisor Programs." Counselors often assist classroom teachers with information for these units and suggest ways to process them with students. The counselors often rotate through these designated times to discuss timely topics such as sexual abuse awareness, sexual harassment policies, and so forth.

It is crucial that all counselors work closely with their faculties to plan times when they can deliver their large group guidance units. We encourage counselors to meet with teachers and find out about the timely issues they feel would be important to include in units. Knowing how to build a strong unit and creating it is exciting, but its actual delivery is the key to knowing how it really affects students. In crowded and limited daily schedules, it is imperative that counselors and their large group guidance units be seen as part of the total curriculum so as not to constantly be fighting for time. Large group units should be scheduled early because of their recognized importance. Units planned and delivered in a haphazard manner will seldom be accepted as important by teachers or administrators.

Delivering the Large Group Guidance Unit

Delivering guidance units are exciting and rewarding experiences. The presenter should be enthusiastic about being in the classroom and excited about what is to be presented. Each lesson can begin with charged energy if the presenter is on time, has planned ahead, and has the content well prepared. We refer to this as beginning a large group session with a "bang"; doing something a little different, maybe even a little "bizarre" or "weird" to get the students' attention.

Successful teachers are knowledgeable about their subject matter, understand it in depth, plan it well, and are also able to deliver the ideas to students in ways they can understand, experience, and process. By the same token, successful, effective school counselors create theoretically sound large group guidance units with exciting age-appropriate activities and present them in ways that the students can understand and benefit from them. Knowledge of subject matter and effective planning cannot be over emphasized. Counselors at all levels need to be aware of large group dynamics and become excellent behavioral managers when they are delivering units. Counselors are often working with established groups or intact classrooms where teachers have already created certain learning climates. Teachers also have evaluative power over students which can help with classroom management. Counselors come into these existing environments and must adapt to them, but also must make them workable situations for their own curriculum delivery. Because counselors do not have to evaluate students when working in the classrooms, students may respond more freely. However, students may also realize that they can act out more since the counselor does not contribute to the grades given. This is why the counselor needs to be aware of large group dynamics and aware of behavioral techniques that are effective in working with large groups.

Marjorie Cuthbert (1993) developed several ideas to help counselors prepare for the delivery of classroom guidance units. She referred to these as the *"Cuthbert Cues."* It is a series of "c" words that helps one to remember different parameters to consider when ensuring all has been attended to in order to assure optimum success. The word "cues" is used as a signal to the counselor to make certain all bases are covered when working with large groups of students or adults. The *"Cuthbert Cues"* include the following dimensions of large group management: (a) *Cohesion,* (b) *Cooperation* (c) *Communication,* (d) *Coaching* (e) *Contribution,* (f) *Control,* (g) *Configuration,* (h) *Closure,* and depending on the topic being discussed, (i) *Confidentiality.*

Cohesion can be built in any group, one that is already in existence or a new one. Begin to establish it quickly by saying: W*e work together and we will plan how we will use our time,* and so forth. Use go-arounds in early sessions where everyone in the group will get to share something about himself or herself, even though it is a large group. Obviously, this cannot be done every time by everyone, because of time constraints. When you know you will be coming back to this particular classroom for more sessions, have a symbol to leave with the group that you can add onto each week (e.g., the school mascot cut out and laminated

Joe Wittmer, Ph.D. and Diane W. Thompson, M.Ed.

works well to post in each room so that a sticky dot can be added to it each week upon the successful completion of a guidance session). Brightly colored folders seem to work well for older students or adults. This reminds them that those who have these folders are all working on the same project. This helps to build group cohesion. In addition, use pairing or *linking statements* often during your delivery. That is, *pair* or *link* the students in both content and feelings as often as possible, i.e., "Bob, you and Jill both really get excited about that concept." *Linking/ pairing* statements help establish cohesion quickly in a large or small group setting.

Cooperation is explained and modeled in groups. You teach group skills to the group by taking turns; listening to others as they will be asked to listen to you; respecting risk-taking and knowing that you will not be laughed at by anyone; and learning how to disagree agreeably. These skills can be practiced and learned. If part of your large group is divided into smaller groups, when the smaller groups are brought back to one large group, you can process how things went in terms of both the groupings and how well cooperation was achieved in both.

Communication is the key element to success for counselors when delivering large group guidance units. Choose a system of communication and practice the suggested skills so that delivering content and eliciting feelings from large groups becomes natural and very rewarding. Myrick and Wittmer (1989) Wittmer (1992, 1993) and Myrick (1993) suggested a continuum of skills that moves from least *facilitative* responses to those most successful in keeping good communication flowing. They suggested using open-ended questions, (those beginning with *what, how, when* or *where*), clarification techniques, and responding with feeling-focused statements which let those to whom you are responding know that you have heard, not only the content of their words, but also have picked up on the underlying feelings. Other techniques suggested by the above mentioned writers are also very useful in maintaining communication flow in large groups. The *"simple acknowledgment"* statement guides you to say *"Thanks"* to a group member for giving out ideas by actually saying the word "Thanks" or something like, "Okay, that's a unique idea" or, "Thanks for sharing that," and then moving on to the next member. And as mentioned, counselors effective as large group leaders also *"pair"* ideas, thoughts, and feelings and *"link"* them with other students' ideas, thoughts, and feelings. As noted, this communication skill contributes heavily to group cohesion.

Coaching is a technique for instilling new behavior by direct instruction and practice with shaping by observers. The group leader or group members help other students by encouraging them to "try out" the presented skills and reinforcing their performance. Large groups work well when counselors teach students that *no one fails* in the group because all other members "*coach*" each other for success. Students also learn how to use the above mentioned facilitative techniques to give helpful feedback to each other which makes participation valuable to members.

Contribution refers to everyone in the group feeling that they have valuable opinions, ideas, or something to give the class. Everyone likes to feel their presence in the lesson is important. You may need to teach volunteering skills to those who are not able to raise their hands, take risks about sharing ideas, and so forth. They may need some added work on deep breathing techniques and positive self-talk, to name just a few. Invite students to help with handing out papers, choosing whether to write on the board or newsprint, or any kind of managerial skills you as the counselor do not need to own.

Control refers to your leadership style in large groups. Are you autocratic, facilitative, permissive? Know yourself and what you can tolerate and what is acceptable to you in terms of the behaviors of the group members. When counselors go into all the different classrooms in their schools, they see all the extremes of leadership styles. It is very important for you to know what works for you and quickly let the group know your style, since they will already have been members in the teachers' systems. Control has to do with not only leadership style, but with classroom techniques such as pacing, varying formats of activities, and being sensitive to ever changing individual behaviors and group behaviors. This permits control techniques to be applied which match the presenting situations. Counselors who present some ideas didactically and then have students role-play, break into smaller discussion groups, or demonstrate ideas with other students as models, and so forth, find these varied activities help control the group and often alleviates the need for disciplinary procedures.

Configuration has to do with room arrangement. Because of time constraints of multiple groups using classrooms in the middle and high schools, or elementary teachers not wanting their own room design varied too much, counselors are asked to work in rooms where the placement of the students' desks and/or tables may not be conducive to the most effective delivery of the guidance unit. Planning ahead with classroom teachers can sometimes help remedy the situation. Since the time the counselor is in the room is so limited, teachers can ask their students to put the room into the configuration the counselor has requested just before the scheduled time for delivery of the unit. This is ideal as lesson time does not have to be devoted to moving desks, charts, and so forth. Time to put the room back for the classroom teacher should be built into each lesson so the courtesy is reciprocated. Classrooms can be structured for success. There are many excellent books available on room configuration with attention given to placements for hard to manage students and how certain configurations enhance learning. How the room is set up and where you place yourself as the group's leader is important to consider as you get ready to deliver large group guidance units.

Joe Wittmer, Ph.D. and Diane W. Thompson, M.Ed.

Closure means giving a summary of what you have learned within the lesson. This is particularly important in that you may not see the same group until the following week or even longer. The closure from a previous lesson serves as review in the next session and helps bring continuity to lessons that are often separated by long periods of time. In the closure section you give the summary and outline plans for next time. This helps insure that the students participating in the large groups look forward to your next lesson.

Confidentiality, or keeping ideas contained within the group, most often comes up in small groups. However, it helps the counselor in large group settings to be aware of the concept and the possibility that the issue might need to be discussed. When counselors create caring, comfortable atmospheres, and discuss issues that conjure up personal experiences, anything can happen in large groups. Students begin to self-disclose very personal perceptions and counselors must attend to the protection of students by addressing confidentiality issues, even in large groups. One counselor has found that making the statement: *Each of us may talk to others about what happened to us (individually) today. However, please do not discuss anything with anyone that happened, or was said by, a fellow student,* as helpful.

As one can observe from the above dimensions of large group management, working with students in large group guidance lessons demands a lot of thought about many concepts, and much energy goes into actual delivery of the units. Managing large group guidance involves not only attending to the content of the units but to the classroom dynamics which are there and ever-changing. Using effective managerial skills when working with large groups adds to the success of such units. There is nothing more exciting than presenting a good classroom guidance unit to students who feel the cohesiveness of the group, cooperate with each other, communicate freely as they coach each other, contribute without fear of being ostracized, and who are in working configurations where control is shared between leader and group. It is an exhilarating experience that is beneficial to the counselor, to many students, and it can be an excellent learning experience for the participating teacher as well.

Summary

Delivering large group developmental guidance is an important dimension of counselors' roles. The format given in this book allows counselors to interact with many students and to impact on their development in a preventative, as opposed to a reactive, manner. They can reach large groups of students with developmental issues or timely topics that need addressing. They can create units to meet specific needs of their populations. Large group guidance is one aspect of the total curriculum which helps counselors know many students. In working with them in large groups, counselors are often able to identify students who might need more individualized attention, either through the small group format or through one-on-one counseling. Presenting large group guidance units also allows counselors to serve as role models for teachers and other professionals who see them managing large groups of students with successful classroom techniques and behavioral interventions. This role strengthens the consultative aspect of the counselor's role, as teachers feel that the counselor is in touch with how to manage students with varying presenting behaviors and will seek consultation for strategies that will assist them in becoming more effective in their own teaching. In tight budget times, delivering developmental guidance units is also an efficient and effective way for students to receive direct service from their counselors and at the same time experience success while participating in a group of their peers.

SECTION I
INTERPERSONAL COMMUNICATION AND COOPERATION

We communicate in many ways and in many different situations. We interact with adults, children, students, teachers, friends, and even strangers with whom we may share only a few brief moments together. We are almost always communicating something to somebody.

The need and desire to communicate and to cooperate with others begins during our first weeks of life. As human beings, we cannot *not* communicate! We are always either saying or implying our ideas, attitudes, or feelings—even when we sit silently.

Think for a moment about the time you spend interacting and talking with others. Many of your daily events involve communication with others. A recent study found that, when awake, we spend more than 60% of our time communicating "one on one" with another human being! Sometimes the experience can be exciting and invigorating, while at other times it may be wearisome and unpleasant.

Communication brings us into cooperative relationships with others. The evidence is clear—we need to interact with other humans and our communication skills determine the outcomes of our interactions. Solitude is often a welcome relief, but most of us do not like much of it. Most people, regardless of cultural background, do not enjoy being alone for extended periods of time. We want to be with people—especially those who listen to us and encourage us to share our thoughts.

One of our greatest human needs is to believe that we are worthwhile and valued individuals. As human beings we seek confirmation about our worth from others. In this sense, we need to establish and maintain close relationships with others. We want to give and receive love. We have a basic need for closeness and also a separateness that acknowledges our uniqueness and self-identity. These essential needs cannot be satisfied without interpersonal communication.

Satisfying interpersonal relationships make us feel good about life and ourselves. Research supports our need for satisfying interpersonal and cooperative relationships and indicates that good interpersonal communication is important to our very survival! Communication and cooperative relationships can influence life style and whether or not we live healthy lives.

Some people may believe that good interpersonal communication is an innate aptitude—something that people are just naturally inclined to be able to do without training. They view communication as a part of being human and the process is inevitable, almost involuntary, like breathing. However, research indicates that most of us do not utilize our potential for communication and that our skill level is far below what it could be.

However, both cooperative and communication skills can be learned. Just as you have learned to read or learned to play a game, you can learn these skills. True, some people may have more aptitude for learning the skills, perhaps as those who have more aptitude in learning music or math, but the skills can be learned.

Each of us has a unique perceptual field. True communication with another is the function of merging two perceptual fields. The two fields must overlap if two-way communication is to occur. When an overlap in perceptual fields occurs, we have accurate understanding and positive identification.

When we think of communication we tend to think of people talking to each other. We think of spoken or written words. They help to transmit meaning and the ability to use them makes us effective communicators. However, communication also occurs at a nonverbal level. Body language is just as important as the words that are used to convey a thought. Our face is one part of our body that reveals feelings. Our eyes, for example, can say many things. They can communicate a warm welcome or an icy attitude. They can invite people to talk more or dismiss them with a disinterested glance.

In this section there are several activities—both verbal and nonverbal—that will aid in the development of communication skills as well as skills that aid in the cooperation with others.

Activity 1.1

The Maligned Wolf:
Understanding Another's Perception

Level: Grades 5 to 12

Purpose: To help students focus on and respect the legitimacy of other people's points of view. To learn a simple clarification response that "lets talkers know you are trying to hear and understand their perceptions."

Materials: *The Maligned Wolf* story.

Activity: Begin by saying: *How many of you have heard the story "Little Red Riding Hood?" Who would like to briefly tell me the story?* (Make sure they mention the evil wolf.) *Have you ever wondered what or how the wolf felt? What do you think the wolf's point of view might have been?*

Next, have someone tell you what *maligned* means. You might have a student use a dictionary; "to slander, to tell untruths." Then, read *The Maligned Wolf* story. Next, lead a discussion concerning the story. Ask: *How did the wolf feel* (misunderstood, depressed, alone, betrayed)?

Next, teach them the clarification response as one way of trying to understand the other person's point of view. You might say: *Any response that is an attempt to acknowledge the content of what a person has said, or to identify the most significant ideas that have been stated, can be termed a **clarifying or summarizing response**. Such statements are helpful when there is some doubt as to whether you're really following the other person's thinking and feeling. In these cases, a clarification statement is a simple way of checking out if what you understood was what the speaker intended. In other situations, clarifying or summarizing responses are deliberately used to help the persons speaking to "hear" what they have said in different words. An accurate response tells others that you have "heard" them.*

When there is a lot of talk in a spontaneous and fast conversation, you cannot expect to understand or grasp everything. Yet, an attempt to let the talker know that you are interested in following what is being said can help facilitate communication between you and the talker.

The clarification statement involves "fresh" (or new) words. It is an attempt to simplify or focus what has been said. Clarifying or summarizing statements focus on the ideas or content of the discussion. This emphasis tends to separate these responses from feeling-focused responses. Clarifying or summarizing responses can give you some "wiggle room."

Ask them to consider the following possible clarifying responses to the wolf. Ask them to complete each statement with fresh words restating, reframing, paraphrasing, and so forth:

If I hear you correctly, you are telling us that....

You seem to be saying, that....

If I am following you, you're saying....

Correct me if I'm wrong, but you're thinking....

Let me see if I understand what you are saying..., you said....

Let's see, your aim was to....

Next, ask the students to practice clarification responses with one another. Place them in small groups of 4 or 5 and ask them to share personal situations of a time when they felt misunderstood.

When they are in their groups say: *In a go-around each member of your group should tell what your misunderstood situation was and how you felt. Then, the person to the left of the talker should attempt to make a clarifying response to the talker.* (Pause, let them do this.) *Now, please focus on the same situation and tell your group what you think the other's person's viewpoint was and how that person felt* (A parent's feelings when you came home two hours late, etc.).

Closure: You might ask: *Who would like to briefly share your misunderstood situations with the whole group? How do you feel when your viewpoint is not understood?* (You might want to jot these feelings on the board.) Then, continue: *We've learned today that both sides of a story can be valid and that we should try to understand what the other's viewpoint is even if we don't agree. If we don't try to understand the others' viewpoint, a lot of unpleasant feelings like feeling misunderstood, hurt, alone, rejected, or even defensiveness can occur in a relationship with that person.*

During this next week pick a well known story and write it from the "bad guy's" viewpoint, i.e., Cinderella's stepmother, the Wolf in the Three Pigs, the witch in Hansel and Gretel. Also, listen carefully to a friend's or family member's story and use clarification responses in trying to tune into them, to see their perception, their view, without judgment and advice.

The Maligned Wolf*

The forest was my home, I lived there and I cared about it. I tried to keep it neat and clean. Then one sunny day, while I was cleaning up some garbage a camper had left behind, I heard footsteps. I leaped behind a tree and saw a rather plain little girl coming down the trail carrying a basket. I was suspicious of this little girl right away because she was dressed funny—all in red—and her head covered up so it seemed like she didn't want people to know who she was. Naturally, I stopped to check her out. I asked who she was, where she was going, where she had come from, and all that. She gave me this song and dance about going to her grandmother's house with a basket of lunch. She appeared to be a basically honest person, but she was in my forest and she certainly looked suspicious with that strange getup of hers. So I decided to teach her just how serious it is to prance through the forest unannounced and dressed funny.

I let her go on her way, but I ran ahead to her grandmother's house. Then I talked to that nice old woman. I explained my problem and she agreed that her granddaughter needed to be taught a lesson. The old woman agreed to stay out of sight until I called her. Actually, she hid under the bed.

When the girl arrived, I invited her into the bedroom where I was in the bed, dressed like the grandmother. The girl came in all rosy-cheeked and said something nasty about my big ears. I've been insulted before so I made the best of it by suggesting that my big ears would help me to hear better. Now, what I meant was that I liked her and wanted to pay close attention to what she was saying. But she made another insulting crack about my bulging eyes. Now you can see how I was beginning to feel about this girl who put on such a nice front, but apparently was a very nasty person. Still, I've made it a policy to turn the other cheek, so I told her that my big eyes helped me to see her better.

Her next insult really got to me. I've got this problem with having big teeth, and that little girl made an insulting crack about them. I know that I should have better control, but I leaped up from that bed and growled that my teeth would help me to eat her better.

Now let's face it. No wolf could ever eat a little girl—everyone knows that—but that crazy girl started running around the house screaming with me chasing her to calm her down. I'd taken off the grandmother's clothes, but that only seemed to make it worse. And all of a sudden, the door came crashing open and a big lumberjack stood there with his ax. I looked at him and all of a sudden I knew that I was in trouble. There was an open window behind me and out I went.

I'd like to say that was the end of it. But the grandmother character never did tell my side of the story. Before long the word got around that I was a mean, nasty guy. Everybody started avoiding me. I don't know about that little girl with the funny red outfit, but I didn't live happily ever after.

*Adapted from Fearn, L. (1974). *The maligned wolf.* San Diego, CA:
Individual Development: Educational Improvement Associates.

Activity 1.2

One- and Two-Way Communication

Level:	Grades 3 to 8
Materials:	Copies of the 3 drawings (each on a separate piece of paper).
Purpose:	To be aware of how communication between people can be one-way or two-way and the impact such communication has on a given task.
Activity:	Begin the activity with a discussion of one- and two-way communication. A lecture, written instructions for a test, and a memo received are familiar examples of one-way communication. A teacher lecturing with one's back to the students while writing on the board during announcements over the public address system is another such example.

Prior to the activity, (on separate pieces of paper) photocopy each of the following three drawings (or draw your own) :

#1

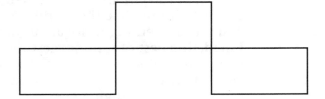

#2

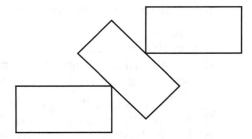

#3

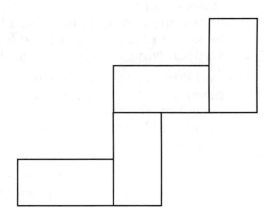

Joe Wittmer, Ph.D. and Diane W. Thompson, M.Ed.

Choose a class member to be the sender. Each student should have a paper and a pencil and be prepared to follow the sender's direction. Hide the sender from view. Give the sender two minutes to describe Figure 1, using any directions desired, in an effort to help the rest of the class draw the figure on their papers. This is one-way communication and there can be no eye contact or questions from the receivers.

Note:

Confusion usually exists at this time and you may want to bring this out in the discussion later. Take note of their behaviors. How did the students react when it became confusing?

When the two minutes are up, ask the receivers to write one or two words on their papers that best describes their feelings at that moment.

Then, let the "sender" show Figure 1 to the receivers and lead a class discussion with a focus on feelings. Unless the sender or receivers are exceptional, very few students will have an accurate drawing of Figure 1. Ask them to discuss how the absence of eye contact affected them, what the notion of "no questions" did to them, and so forth. How did the sender feel? Talk about the importance of eye contact in the general American culture and how we use our eyes to communicate with others.

Begin a second round by choosing a new sender. Give the sender Figure 2 and repeat the above procedures. (Hide the sender.) However, the receivers, as a group, may ask five questions during this two-minute period. You will notice that this drawing is somewhat more difficult than Figure 1. However, because of the two-way interaction, more students will draw it accurately. Discuss the round. Again, discuss the lack of face-to-face eye contact in our everyday communication with others.

Select a different sender for the third round and give that person two minutes to describe Figure 3. Do not hide the sender and allow as much interaction as possible between the sender and the receivers during the two-minute time limit. Although this drawing is much more difficult to describe, greater accuracy in the receivers' drawings will generally result. Some senders might be more frustrated with Figure 3 than with Figure 1 because two-way communication takes longer and requires more patience. (Discuss this concept.) It's easy to tell someone how to do something. It is also quicker but is seldom "understood" unless there is two-way interaction. However, the receivers usually feel more confident with Figures 2 and 3 than with Figure 1.

Closure:

Lead a discussion on one-way and two-way communication and the impact both types have on us as human beings. *Did eye contact make a difference? How did seeing the sender make a difference? How did being permitted to ask questions affect your ability as a receiver (to complete the drawings)? What did you learn today that can be applied to "everyday" conversations?*

Activity 1.3

Asking the Appropriate Questions to Improve Communication

(A variation of the previous activity)

Level: Grades 6 to 12

Purpose: To demonstrate how asking the appropriate questions enhances two-way communication, especially when asking open-ended questions.

Materials: Paper and pencil. Individual copies of Figures 1, 2, 3, and 4.

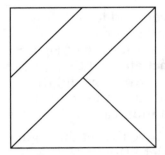 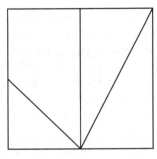 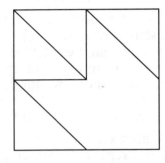 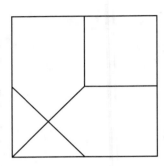

Figure 1   Figure 2   Figure 3   Figure 4

Activity I: Begin by telling the students that you are going to begin by playing "twenty questions" with a "twist"—they can't ask any questions. Tell them that you are thinking of an animal and have them guess what it is. (Select an uncommon animal that they're unlikely to guess.) Remind the group: *Remember, no questions will be answered regarding the type of animal I'm thinking about."*

Ask: *What was it like to try and figure out what animal I was thinking of?* (frustrating) *What made it difficult to guess the animal?* (not being able to ask questions)

Activity II: Ask the group to divide a piece of paper into four sections. (Fold in half twice.) Let them know that in each of the sections they will be drawing figures which will be "communicated to them in different ways."

For section one, have a student hidden (behind a portable chalkboard, or whatever) so that student can only be heard and not seen. Have the "hidden" student verbally describe Figure 1 while the others attempt to draw it. Do not allow any questions (expect a lot of frustration).

After about 3 or 4 minutes, show Figure 1 to the students.

Ask: *What hindered you in effectively drawing this diagram?* (Not being able to ask questions.) *What helped in communicating how to draw this diagram?* (some talking) *What was it like trying to draw the diagram?* (frustrating, difficult)

Joe Wittmer, Ph.D. and Diane W. Thompson, M.Ed.

For section two of their paper, have a student stand in front of the group and verbally describe Figure 2 while the students attempt to draw it. Allow closed-questions only. (Questions that solicit a one word answer such as "yes" or "no.")

After about 3 or 4 minutes, show Figure 2 to the students.

Ask: *What kept you from drawing the diagram correctly?* (The answers to the questions gave very little information.) *What helped you to draw this diagram somewhat better than Figure 1?* (Being able to ask questions, seeing the person's non-verbal cues, etc.) *What was it like trying to draw this diagram?* (Frustrating, a little easier than Figure 1.)

For section three of their papers, have a student stand in front of the group and verbally describe Figure 3. Allow two open-ended questions only. (Open-ended questions which solicit more than a one word response beginning with what, how, when, or where.) Give the students some examples of open-ended questions.

Examples:

What does the diagram look like?

How do the squares in the diagram fit together?

Show Figure 3 to the students. Ask: *What made it easier for the diagram to be communicated so that you might draw it better?* (Seeing the non-verbal cues, being able to ask the type questions that gained much information, etc.) *What made it difficult for the diagram to be communicated?* (Only 2 questions permitted.)

For section four, on their papers have a student stand in front of the group and verbally describe Figure 4. Allow for as many open-ended questions as the students want to ask.

Allow 3 or 4 minutes and then show Figure 4 to the students. Ask: *What made drawing this diagram easier than the other 3?* (Being able to ask as many questions as we wanted, lots of information was given in response to questions, etc.) *What made it still somewhat difficult to draw the diagram?* (Couldn't see it.) *If you don't understand something, what can you do to get the most information?* (Ask an open-ended question—one that begins with what, how, when, or where!)

Activity III: Practice open-ended questions by having the students play twenty-questions (open-ended questions only) while one student thinks of an animal, plant, or object. The other students ask open-ended questions (what, how, when, or where) and attempt to guess.

Closure: Say something like: *We have learned today that if we need more information communicated to us, we should ask open-ended questions which give us more than one word answers. In addition, asking others open-ended questions shows them that you are truly interested in them and what they have to say. For example, if I ask you, "Did you enjoy this activity today?" (closed question) you can simply answer "yes" or "no." However, notice the difference when I ask, "What did you like or dislike about today's activity?" This shows that I'm inviting your response and that I'm interested in your response.*

Activity 1.4

The Johari Window*

Level:	Grades 6 to 12
Materials:	Overhead of the Johari Window and a copy for each student.
Purpose:	For students to explore their values and personal characteristics and how these relate to their communication styles.
Activity:	You might begin by saying: *Your willingness to disclose, or not to, as well as listen to feedback from others has a great deal to do with your understanding of yourself as well as other's understanding of you.*

Inform the students that the Johari Window is a good model to use when you want to look at yourself. That is, it will help you discover more about yourself and how you communicate with others. Next, flash the Johari Window on the screen (or draw on the board), give each student a copy, and explain the four areas of the window.

Area I: Let the students know that the Johari window is a framework for defining your self-concept. You might say: *Area I, the free area, includes everything you know and understand about yourself and all that other people know and understand about you—your values, personality characteristics, and perceptions. For example, you may enjoy wearing very nice clothes and so you spend lots of time and money on your wardrobe. This is easily communicated to others through the clothes you wear. Others, in turn, are aware of your enjoyment of wearing such clothing because they observe what you wear.* Ask for other examples from the students.

Area II: Explain Area II as follows: *The blind area, Area II, represents all those things about you that others recognize but that you do not see in yourself. You may, for example, make a poor first impression on certain people because you are loud and obnoxious. Unless this behavior is pointed out to you, it will remain in the blind area and detract from the effectiveness of your communication. Information in the blind area is revealed only when you have the opportunity to investigate other people's perceptions of you. Unfortunately, problems can arise in your relationships with others if you do not know about these important aspects of yourself.* Again, ask the students for additional examples.

Area III: You might explain Area III as follows: *In the hidden area, Area III, you recognize something about yourself but choose not to share it with others. If you are a male, for example, you may have learned not to show certain types of emotions, such as crying; yet you sometimes face situations in which crying would express your true feelings. It seems necessary to you to control yourself so as to avoid an 'unmanly' display of tears.* Ask for other examples and lead a discussion on Area III.

*Luft, J. (1969). *Of human interaction*. Palo Alto, CA: National Press Books.

Area IV:

You might say: *The unknown area, Area IV, represents all those things that neither you nor others know about you. If you do not sit down and analyze who you are, why you act the way you do, or what internal drives trigger or control your actions, many aspects of yourself may remain unknown. Often they are so well concealed that they never even surface to the conscious level. These aspects remain unknown not only to you, but to everyone else. They can inspire you to take certain actions and participate in certain activities, yet you are unaware of the part they play in your life. For example, in therapy you may suddenly remember that you were sexually abused as a child. This may explain a strong aversion to being touched.* Again, request examples from the students.

Activity:

Ask each student to list a personal characteristic, a value, or whatever, in Areas 1 and 3 (and perhaps 2 and 4—a guess) and ask for volunteers to share with the rest of the class or in triads.

Closure:

Explain to the students that almost no one finds that all the panels in his or her window are of equal size. For example, people who are very open and easily share themselves with others normally have a small free area and a large, hidden, and unknown area. Lead a discussion on this concept.

You may want to close by saying: *You may want to use the Johari Window to very carefully analyze yourself. Consider the four areas and determine which may be most dominant in your communication patterns, especially in your self-communication. Being honest in your self-assessment will reveal a great deal about yourself and it may even cause you some pain. Which area is largest in your Johari Window? Is one area the most dominant? If your window reflects a very open, free individual (that is, an extremely large Area I), your communication patterns are quite different from those of a person with a very large Area III. That person probably speaks less, attempts to conceal his or her real feelings, and avoids opportunities to tell it like it is.*

Johari Window

	Known to Self	Not Known to Self
Known to Others	1. Free Area	2. Blind Area
Not Known to Others	3. Hidden Area	4. Unknown Area

Joe Wittmer, Ph.D. and Diane W. Thompson, M.Ed.

Activity 1.5

Communication—What is It?*

(First Activity in a sequence of four activities)

Level: Grades 3 to 8

Purpose: To learn a basic definition of communication and to distinguish unclear communication from clear communication.

Materials: Paper and pencils.

Activity I: Discuss and teach the meaning of the word "communication." Discuss how communication involves: a) sending a message and b) receiving a message. This may best be done by drawing a picture on the board to illustrate the point; i.e., a picture of a TV station sending a message via a satellite dish to an orbiting satellite which sends it to a backyard satellite dish (the receiver of the message) into a TV set in the home. Relate this to how we humans communicate.

Next, emphasize how people are always communicating by sending messages and receiving messages. *We cannot not communicate. We are always "saying" something, giving a message, even when we're quiet. We do not need words to send messages. Just by the way we walk or sit or look at others is sending a message.*

Ask the students to guess what messages you are trying to send as you demonstrate the following exaggerated facial expressions and postures:

- Frowning, hands on hips to communicate **anger**.
- Smiling broadly and jumping up and down to communicate **happiness**.
- Eyebrows raised, arms crossed to communicate **disapproval**.
- Hands across mouth, eyes wide open to communicate **fear**.
- Clenching fists, smiling broadly to show **excitement**.

Ask the students if the things you just demonstrated were **clear** or **unclear** communication. Even though the medium was non-verbal, most students (unless from a foreign country) will clearly understand your messages.

Ask: *What is clear communication?*

Answer: The message that one person sends clearly is the same message the other person receives: Communication is a two-way street.

Unclear Communication: Ask the students to guess what messages you are now trying to send as you demonstrate the following mixed messages (usually these are quite humorous):

- Hands on hips, angry facial expression while saying, "I am really very happy today."_____
- Broad smile, jumping up and down saying, "I am so angry."
- Pound the table and say, "I am not angry."
- Shake your head "no" while saying "yes."

* This sequence of four activities was adapted from: Cihak, M.K. & Heron, J. (1980). *Games children should play.* Glenview, IL: Scott, Foresman.

Say something like: *Sometimes the message I send is not the one you receive because I may not be sending it clearly. Or, sometimes I may be sending it clearly, but you may not be receiving because your "radar" is receiving communication from somewhere else. That is, you're not tuned in to me.*

Ask the students to give examples of times when communication has been/is unclear at home, at school, and so forth.

Say something like: *Misunderstandings can occur when people think they have received the message clearly, but they really have not understood it. A way to be sure you have received the correct message is to ask the person who sent it some questions which "invite" more information regarding what they just said. Begin your questions with "what," "how," "when," or "where."*

Then, conduct role playing of clear and unclear communication. Either read directly (or organize role plays) to demonstrate one or more of the sample situations that follow below. Ask the following questions after each role play (or direct reading of the situation as you develop it):

  a. *What was the message?*

  b. *What about the communication that made it clear or unclear?*

  c. *What did you notice about the listener?*

  d. *What could the listener have done to have listened more carefully?*

The following situations may lend themselves to varied interpretations. Take time to discuss the reasoning behind the students' responses. Encourage divergent student responses to the above four (a-d) questions (so long as they are reasonable and realistic).

The Role Play Situations

1. A teacher explains a math problem while the class listens carefully and obviously understands the directions on how to solve the problem.

2. The teacher tells a joke. One student turns to another and grins. That student frowns. (You may need to point out again that communication often takes place without words.)

3. Two people talk in the hall. One person shouts, "I won't do that," and walks away. The other person shrugs his or her shoulders.

4. A man stops at a service station and asks directions to Maple Street. The service station attendant says, "Oh, you go about three or four—maybe more—blocks down this way, then you turn right and a little way down that street you'll see a white house. Turn left and there's Maple Street."

5. A teenager watches a gourmet cook on television and bakes a cake

according to the directions she hears. "This cake tastes different," she thinks. That night her mother says, "The cake tastes like salt. How much salt did you use? "Two cups," says the teenager. "The cook on TV should have added sugar instead of all that salt. It would have been sweeter," the teenager says.

6. Two friends have a bad argument. One friend calls the other and says, "I feel terrible about our fight. I'd like to be friends again." "I feel that way, too," says the other person. "Let's walk to school together tomorrow."

7. The quarterback tries to explain the next play to the team. Everyone runs off in different directions and the play is ruined.

8. The teacher explains long division to the class. One student is watching a softball game outside the window. When the teacher finishes the explanation and asks, "Does everyone understand?" The boy watching the softball game shakes his head and asks for another lesson in long division.

Activity II:

Next, play the "Silly Sentences" Game. Have each student take out a piece of paper and a pencil. At the top of the page each student should write an adjective. (With younger students, you may have to explain an adjective as a word describing a thing.) Then, have each student fold down the top of the page to hide the word each has just written and then pass it on to another student. Now, have all students write a noun on the paper they've just had passed to them and then fold the paper again so as to also hide the second word. Continue the passing, writing, folding sequence until five (5) words (making a sentence) have been written. The sequence of words should be as follows:

> first word - adjective
>
> second word - noun
>
> third word - verb
>
> fourth word - adverb
>
> fifth word - prepositional phrase

When the "silly sentences" are complete, allow all participants to read them out loud. Then ask: *Do the sentences make sense?* (no) *Why was the sentence an example of unclear communication? What could we have done to make the communication more clear?*

Optional:

If time permits, you might play the game again, this time allowing the students to view the word(s) the students before them wrote on the paper.

Closure:

Say something like: *We have learned today that communication is the sending and receiving of messages. In addition, we've learned that the message can be misunderstood because of unclear sending or unclear receiving. Next time we will discuss how clear communication takes more than just cleaning your ears out every morning.*

Activity 1.6

What Did You Say?

(Second of a four activity sequence)

Level: Grades 3 to 8

Purpose: To help the students to realize that listening well (receiving messages) and speaking clearly (sending messages) can be difficult and takes concentration, and a willingness to learn the specific skills of "sending" and "receiving" messages.

Materials: Paper and pencil.

Activity: Review the definition of communication from last time (sending and receiving messages) and then let the group know that they will be practicing sending and receiving messages today.

Next, have 5 or 6 students (perhaps selecting one row in the class) step outside the classroom. The rest of the class, with your help, should come up with a "wild" made-up short story. Have a member of the class record the main (briefly) details of the story.

Ask one of the students you've sent outside to come in and tell that person the classes' story. That person, in turn, tells the next student who comes in, who in turn, tells the next student, and so forth. By the time the last student tells the story, it is usually mixed up, very unclear, with many details missing.

Next, ask: *What was the problem?* (Students were either not receiving clearly or sending clearly.)

Play a few more rounds of the game allowing all students to participate and encouraging them to really focus when receiving the story and being clear when sending the signal to the next student.

Then, ask the students: *If all of us were to be silent, would there be anything to listen to?* or, *Does a falling tree make a sound if no one is there to hear it fall?* Some students will say no. Continue by explaining if we really focus on listening, there are always things we can hear or receive. Ask them to tune into the other sounds they are currently hearing in the room.

Demonstrate this point by having all students be as quiet as possible for three minutes. Use your watch. (This will seem like a long time for most students.) While they are being quiet, have them write down everything they hear. It may help to open a window or a door. For younger students, you may want to offer a small prize (sticker) to anyone who hears 10 or more different sounds.

Closure: Say something like: *We have shown today how communication can be difficult if the sending and receiving of messages is unclear. One way to receive messages more clearly is to focus and concentrate on listening. Some people call it listening with the third ear. It takes skill to tune out stuff you don't want to interfere with what you want to tune in to. Next time we will talk about and practice listening skills.*

Activity 1.7

I Heard You the First Time

(Third activity in sequence of four)

Level: Grades 3 to 8

Purpose: To demonstrate and practice good listening skills.

Materials: Listen Quiz and Ten Guidelines for Effective Listening (a copy for each student).

Activity I: **Demonstration of Poor listening and Good Listening.** Ask for a volunteer to come to the front of the group and then sit face-to-face with the volunteer. Have that person share something he or she really likes to do after school. As the student is talking, you should exhibit poor listening, i.e., look away, get up, lean back, cross your arms. After a minute stop and ask: *Was I listening to_____ (name of student)?* (No!) *What kinds of things was I doing which indicated that I wasn't listening?* (Getting up, not looking at the person speaking, etc.)

Ask for another volunteer to come to the front of the group and have that person share with you about what he or she likes to do after school. This time exhibit good listening skills (keeping still, leaning a bit forward, remain on same level, eye contact, etc.).

Ask: *Was I listening this time?* (Yes) *What was I doing that indicated I was listening?* (Squaring shoulders, eye contact, keeping still, leaning forward, appearing interested, remaining on same level, etc.)

Activity II: **Listening Practice.** Have the students pair up and sit face-to-face. Explain that they are going to practice good listening posture as their partner speaks for one minute on a topic you will assign. Then, they will be sharing (the same topic) while their partners listen to them.

Suggested Topics:
- A good dream I had...
- A place I'd like to visit...
- What I'd do with a million dollars...
- What I did this past weekend...

(It would be helpful to have a bell to ring or some such device to signal the end of each minute when the partners should switch roles.)

Bring the group back together and ask:

- *How well did you listen?*
- *How well did you feel your partner listened?*
- *How did it feel to be listened to?*
- *How did it feel to listen carefully to someone else?*
- Pass out the "Listen Quiz" to all students. Ask them to have a pencil ready to use.
- Say to the students something like: *This exam will be a good way for us to review what we have learned today about listening. Together we are going to decide if some sentences are true or false.*

Read the Listen Quiz statements aloud and have the class determine whether they are Yes or No. If the sentence fits, have them place a large "Y" in the blank preceding the sentence. If No, they should place an "N" in the space.

Have the students form triads and share their answer to the Quiz.

Closure:

Close by conducting a go-around asking each student to complete this sentence: *I learned or relearned _____ today about listening.* Optional for higher level grades: The "Ten Guidelines for Effective Listening" found at the end of this activity.

Joe Wittmer, Ph.D. and Diane W. Thompson, M.Ed.

The Listen Quiz

_____ 1. Does a good listener look directly into the eyes of the person who is speaking?

_____ 2. Does a good listener think about other things while listening?

_____ 3. Is a noisy, crowded place with lots of distractions a good place to try to carefully listen to another?

_____ 4. Does a good listener lean a bit forward when listening to someone?

_____ 5. Is facing toward the speaker a sign of a good listener?

_____ 6. Does a good listener's face show he or she is interested while listening?

_____ 7. Does a good listener stand up and move around while the speaker is sitting?

_____ 8. Does a good listener turn away from the person who is speaking?

_____ 9. Does a good listener listen better while jumping up and down?

_____ 10. Can anyone without physical hearing problems be a good listener if one chooses to be?

_____ 11. Listening is natural and does not require skills?

_____ 12. Tuning out sounds other than the speaker is easy and does not require concentrating?

Ten Guidelines for Effective Listening

1. STOP TALKING!

   You cannot listen if you are talking. Focus on the verbal and nonverbal behavior of the speaker, not on what you want to say (Out focus).

2. PUT THE TALKER AT EASE.

   Help a person feel free to talk by being non-judgmental. Listen to understand rather than to oppose.

3. SHOW A TALKER THAT YOU WANT TO LISTEN.

   Remove distractions, give undivided attention.
   Eye contact.
   Body language.
   Verbal following; no changing the subject.

4. EMPATHIZE WITH TALKERS.

   Try to understand the other person's point of view.
   Listen and respond to feelings as well as content.

5. BE PATIENT.

   Allow plenty of time.
   Do not interrupt.
   Non-verbal behavior should reflect patience.

6. CHECK YOUR EMOTIONS.

   You stop listening when your emotions begin to control you!
   An angry person takes the wrong meaning from words.

7. GO EASY ON ARGUMENT, CRITICISM, AND ADVICE-GIVING.

   This puts people on the defensive and they may "clam up" or become angry. Do not argue! Even if you win, you lose. Do not lecture or try to persuade to your point of view.

8. GO EASY ON REASSURANCE.

   Speaker wants to be heard not told what they should feel or think. Premature reassurance closes the conversation.

9. ASK OPEN-ENDED QUESTIONS.

   Helps the speaker continue to explore thoughts and feelings and develop points further.
   Shows you are listening.

10. CHECK FOR ACCURACY OF YOUR PERCEPTIONS.

    Say back in your own words what you heard the speaker say.
    The speaker has the opportunity to clarify and correct the message.
    The speaker has the opportunity to reexamine the message.
    Helps assure accuracy and full understanding of thoughts and feelings. Helps the speaker examine more fully, develop points further.

Activity 1.8

So That's How You Feel!

(Fourth of a four activity sequence)

Level:	Grades 3 to 8
Purpose:	To demonstrate to students that listening to the feelings being expressed by others, as well as the content of their messages, facilitates clearer communication. In addition, they learn that skills, which take practice, are needed to effectively "tune in to" the feelings of others.
Materials:	None.
Activity I:	Begin by saying to the students: *Last time we did an activity together during which we practiced listening. Today we are going to go one step further by listening for the feelings as well as listening to what the speaker is saying. What is a feeling? Are feelings pleasant or unpleasant?* (First, write a list on the board under a column labeled pleasant.)

What feelings can you name that are unpleasant? (Write a list on the board under the column labeled unpleasant.)

Here are some sample words:

Pleasant	**Unpleasant**
Brave	Afraid
Calm	Bored
Cheerful	Confused
Happy/Glad	Depressed
Confident	Disappointed
Excited	Mad
Nice	Lonely
Pleased	Jealous
Proud	Sad
Relieved	Tired
Strong	Worried
Surprised	Hurt

Activity II: Begin by saying: *We are going to play a game in which you have to listen to what the person is saying and feeling. Let's try a few examples together.*

Read the following examples aloud and have the students respond to what kind of feelings the person was having. That is, were they pleasant or unpleasant? Then, have them "label" the feeling(s) they hear. They may want to refer to the list above.

1. "A terrible thing happened to me last Sunday. I had invited my best friends to come for dinner and just as I was finishing preparations for the big celebration, my phone rang. It was my friends calling. They said their car had broken down and they couldn't come after all." (Sad, disappointed, lonely, depressed, etc.)

2. "I've started a new hobby. A friend of mine showed me all about stamp collecting and now I have several books of stamps. I found out just last week that my stamp collection is worth a lot more money now than when I first bought those stamps. Besides the money the stamps are worth, I really like to look at them because they are so beautiful." (Happy, proud, secure, etc.)

3. "When I was going on summer vacation, I packed my suitcase real full of all my best clothes, my favorite books, and some nice gifts for my friends. When I got to my destination, I looked and looked for the suitcase at the airport, but I could not find it. It was lost somewhere. It had not been put on the airplane." (Angry, irritated, upset, unhappy, etc.)

4. "I saw a movie on television a few nights ago. When I started watching it I didn't know what kind of movie it was going to be. I couldn't watch until the end because I was afraid I would not have good dreams. I locked up my windows very tight that night and checked all the doors to be sure they were locked." (Afraid, uneasy, etc.)

Activity III:

Divide the group into two teams. Have one student from each team come to the front of the class and sit facing each other. Ask one team member to secretly pick and then whisper to you one of the feelings off of the feelings list and tell a short story about time he or she felt that way without using that particular feeling word.

The opposing team member tries to guess which feeling word the person has chosen to demonstrate. Remind them to think of them as being pleasant, unpleasant or perhaps both.

Award one point to the team each time they guess a feeling correctly.

Continue playing by switching which team tells the story and which team guesses the feeling. Allow everyone in the group a chance to participate.

Closure:

Say something like: *It is very important to listen for feelings as well as words, because it allows for much clearer communication. Remember to practice tuning into the feelings of others. Also, remember to think in terms of pleasant, unpleasant, or both as the speaker is talking.*

Activity 1.9

Working Together

(Adapted from an activity submitted by Ashley Wiest)

Level:

Grades K to 1

Purpose:

To help younger students learn the value of working together to accomplish a specific goal.

Materials:

5 pieces of thick string, yarn, or rope (6 to 8 feet in length each)

Activity:

Have the students pair up and sit on the floor, back to back with their knees bent and elbows linked. On the count of three, each pair tries to stand up. Have the children practice in pairs on their own once or twice more, before moving on to sets of three. The game continues by trying to stand up with three, then four, five, six, and more people. Depending on the group's experience, determine when the game should end.

Next, lead a discussion around the following questions: *What did you like/dislike about this game? How were you and your partner able to stand up together? What did you each do to make this happen? What does the word "cooperation" mean?* (Working together, sharing, etc.) *What happened when you fell down or couldn't stand up?*

What was it like when another joined you? What made standing up difficult?

Next, divide the class into groups of five. Then:

1. Give each group a length of string.

2. Have every member of the group hold part of the string.

3. Call out the name of a shape for the groups to form, while holding onto the string. Start with a simple circle.

4. Allow the groups to talk while forming the circle, but then have the students try to make other shapes, (i.e., triangle, square, rectangle, star) or letters (L,C,V,W,M,N,J,Z, etc.) without talking.

5. After time in smaller groups, bring the students together into two large groups. Tie the strings together and try making the shapes with more people.

Then, lead a brief discussion on the following questions:

- *What did you like/dislike about this activity?*
- *What did your group do to make the shape (or letter)?*
- *What does it mean to "cooperate" when you are playing a game?*
- *What did you do when you were not allowed to talk?*
- *What kinds of problems did you run into? How did you solve them?*
- *How did it feel when someone was not cooperating with the group?*

Closure:

Lead a closing discussion around the following:

- *When are some other times you work together (cooperate) with people?*
- *Tell about a time when you "cooperated" with someone in class (with a family member, with a friend).*
- *How do you feel when you "cooperate" with others?*
- *What happens when we do not cooperate with each other?*

Activity 1.10

Cooperation

Level:	Grades K to 12
Purpose:	Students will define "cooperation" and experience activities which require cooperation.
Materials:	Masking tape.
Activity:	Begin by holding up a large sign with the word "cooperation." Give examples of people cooperating to achieve a common goal. Have the students come up with their own definition (their age level) of cooperation.

Play the following cooperation games emphasizing how working together is the only way to "win."

a. "SIT DOWN CIRCLE:" Have the students stand in a circle, front to back. On the count of "three," all students sit down slowly on the person's lap behind him or her. They have to work together to keep from falling. (You might wish to separate males and females for this activity.)

b. "STAND UP CIRCLE:" Have four students sit on the floor, back to back. Tell them to lock arms. At the count of "three," they are to attempt to stand up without unlinking arms.

c. "KNOTS:" Have 6 to 8 students hold hands in a straight line. Without letting their hands go, have the group "tie up in a knot." Have them work together to "get out of the knot" and back into a straight line.

d. "WALKING THE LINE:" Place a line of masking tape on the floor. Have three students stand at each end of the line. Have one student from each end walk toward each other. Their task is to help each other pass one another while not stepping off the line.

Closure:	Ask 2 or 3 students to sum up what they learned about cooperation, or if time permits, do a go-around with each student completing the following statement: "I learned or relearned today that...."

Joe Wittmer, Ph.D. and Diane W. Thompson, M.Ed.

Activity 1.11

Data Processing

Level: Grades 3 to 12

Purpose: For students to play a game that encourages communication and helps them to learn more about each other.

Materials: None.

Activity I: You might say: *Today we're going to learn some interesting facts about each other through a great game!* Divide the group into two teams that will compete against each other or have the whole group work together as a team against the clock. Tell the students: *The object of the game is to get the team into the proper order, ranking, or sequence in the shortest amount of time. I will call out a certain order and then when the team thinks that they're in the right order everyone sit or squat down. Let's try an example. Get in order from shortest to tallest!* Time them or see which team finishes first. Check to make sure they are in the correct order. Keep score by awarding the team that sits down first five points or just keep track of the amount of time the team takes to get in to the order you request.

Suggestions for sequences:

1. Alphabetical order by first names/last names/middle names.
2. Numerical order by age (including months).
3. Alphabetical order by state born in/city born in.
4. Alphabetical order by favorite ice cream.
5. In order of your birth month as it comes in the year.
6. In alphabetical order by names of favorite hobbies.

MAKE UP YOUR OWN!

Closure: You may want to ask each student to share something new he or she learned about another person from the game.

Activity 1.12

Communication Between the Sexes

Level: Grades 7 to 12

Purpose: To facilitate communication between males and females; to heighten awareness of sex role stereotypes.

Materials: None.

Activity: First, form two circles, one circle within another. The females sit in the inside circle while the males sit on the outside.

For the first ten minutes the females are encouraged to talk about males, venting their unpleasant and pleasant feelings. What are their pet peeves? How do they think males their age see females? The outer circle (males) participants observe, but do not participate in the inner group discussion in any manner whatsoever.

After about ten minutes, the circles are reversed, with the males on the inside responding to the same questions and tasks.

Then, bring both groups together in one large circle and discuss how they felt about the activity and what they learned from it. You or the group members might pose additional questions.

Variations:

a. The females sit in the inside circle and pretend they are males and males (later) pretend they're female. They talk about how it feels to be "male" or "female" and what they like and dislike about their sex and the role society expects them to play. They might also talk about how they see females (males) or talk about, "Things I like and dislike about being a girl or boy," or "Things that I would like to change in our society in terms of being masculine or feminine." Each group might be encouraged to talk about the biggest problem of the opposite sex in today's society.

b. The males write statements about what it feels like to be a boy and some of their likes and dislikes. The statements are then given to the circle of females, who read them and respond. For example, "My girlfriend makes me feel cheap when I can't afford to take her to some places," or, "Why do boys always have to be the ones to set up a date?" or "I like a girl, but she doesn't like me." The females could then write statements of what it's like being a female and the boys could respond.

Closure: Lead a discussion on gender equity issues in our society and how such issues impact both males and females.

Activity 1.13

Line Up

Level:	Grades 6 to 12
Purpose:	To build group cohesion by having students cooperate in completing a group task without the aid of speech (no talking whatsoever).
Materials:	Blind folds, one for each group member.
Activity:	You might begin by saying: *If you have ever been responsible for organizing a group to perform a task, you know it can be difficult. What if you had to organize a group, but no one in the group, not even you, could speak? You would be forced to find other ways to communicate. Let's try it by playing "Line Up."*

Move the class into teams of 5 or 6 each. Have each group pick a leader and then have one group come to the center of the room while the others watch. Then say: *Everyone except the leader should put on a blindfold—no peeping! Be absolutely quiet!* The leader then whispers a different number, from one through the number in the group, to each person in your group. The leader should use each number only once.

The team's group task is to line up in numerical order with NO talking. Leader reports when the group has completed their task. When task is complete and all are in line numerically, remove blindfolds and return to seats. Then move another group into the center of the room to carry out the same task until all groups have played "Line Up."

Closure:	*What did you learn from Line Up? Could the line have been formed without everyone's cooperation? Was the group slowed down by anyone's failure to cooperate?* Close by leading a discussion on how it is often necessary to cooperate in order to get tasks accomplished and our needs met.

Activity 1.14

The Year 3000

Level:	Grades 3 to 9
Purpose:	To enhance communication among students regarding their personal values.
Materials:	Pictorial magazines, scissors, and colored construction paper.
Activity:	First, divide the class into groups of around five and appoint a recording secretary for each group. The task for each group is to put together a time capsule that will fully describe their particular group (their ages) to people who will be living 1,000 years from now. That is, they are to describe themselves (today's youth) so as to be "understood" by future society.

Then, tell each group that they must decide on:

    a. four musical recordings

    b. five magazine pictures

    c. an original paragraph, poem, or short story

    d. four significant events of the past five years that best depicts them today and will best describe their particular group to people who will be living 1,000 years from now

       ("c" and "d" may need to be modified for younger children.)

The five magazine pictures could be pasted or taped to a piece of construction paper. After each group has decided on its four recordings, its pictures, and the historical events, they may add two more "things" to their respective time capsule that the group members would like to see added. Then, in turn, have the recording secretaries report and show the class the time capsules.

Closure:	Next, have the class, as a group, decide on one capsule to best represent the class. You may want to use the democratic process in making the decision. Hold a discussion on the "message" about our "values" being sent by the contents for the time capsule to be "dug up" in the year 3000.

Activity 1.15

Conflict: What Is It?

Level:	Grades 5 to 12
Purpose:	To learn one's personal style of dealing with conflict and to learn some effective methods for dealing with personal conflict.
Materials:	Large typed signs (the **Turtle**, the **Shark**, the **Teddy Bear**, and the **Owl**) to post in the corners of the room, and the "Four C's" handout.
Activity:	Introduce the concept of conflict by having the students share some of their ideas about what conflict is. Help the class develop a definition. For example, a conflict is when you and another person disagree and continue to argue your own respective points of view. It is usually where you find yourself with an opposite or very different opinion and the clash is great. Conflicts can be expressed verbally and/or physically.

Next, ask for examples of conflict. Ask about conflicts between friends, families, within oneself, between teachers and students, between countries, and so forth. Lead a short discussion on:

- What kinds of things cause conflicts?
- What makes a conflict worse?
- *What makes a conflict better?*

Then say: *Each one of us has different ways of handling conflicts. There are "TYPES" in conflict resolution. I have four "TYPES" to describe to you. As I read these, try to see which type describes you* (realizing there is overlap). *Then, after I finish reading each of the four descriptions, move to the area of the room where your type is posted.*

Conflict Resolution Types

THE TURTLE: Turtles try to avoid conflict by pulling their heads into their shells or withdrawing. When they see conflict they try to stay away from getting involved. They believe that conflicts really can't be solved. They are always willing to give up their personal goals and friendships to avoid conflicts. That is, they just "pull their heads" into their shells, give in, and will not "stand their ground."

THE SHARK: Sharks deal with conflict by forcing the other person to agree with them. Since their goals are more important to them than their friendships, they seldom care about the needs or feelings of the other person in the conflict. Winning a conflict gives them a sense of pride and achievement. Losing a conflict makes them feel weak and not OK. They have a very high need to avoid losing and view it as personal failure.

THE TEDDY BEAR: Teddy Bears want to be loved and have others love them. They try to avoid conflict at all costs so they will be accepted and liked by everyone. They give up their belief in things that are important to them just so people will continue to like them.

THE OWLS: Owls see conflict as problems that can be solved in ways that make each person in the conflict feel OK. They see working through a conflict to a satisfactory conclusion as a way of improving the friendship. They are not satisfied until both parties' needs are met and they both feel good about the solution. They also often find themselves mediating conflicts that occur between others.

Give the students in each corner an opportunity to hold a five or ten minute discussion among themselves. What is it about themselves that brought each to that particular corner of the room?

Then ask the students what *type* they would like to be and ask them to move to that corner of the room. Allow five minutes for the "new" participants in each corner to hold a discussion with other students in that particular corner.

For a final activity have the students break into groups of five and share a conflict they experienced in or out of school. Have them describe how they handled the situation. *What was the outcome and how would they handle it differently in the future? Which one of the four "types" were they revealing when they handled the situation and which "type" would they have revealed had they handled it differently?*

Closure:

Bring the small groups back into the larger group and lead a discussion on the Four C's handout. (Pass out the handout prior to beginning the discussion.)

RULE OF THE FOUR C'S*

WHEN FACED WITH A DIFFICULT SITUATION, REMEMBER THE RULE OF THE FOUR C'S. *CONCERN, CONFER, CONSULT, CONFRONT.* ALWAYS START WITH THE C, *CONCERN.* IS THIS SITUATION A MATTER OF REAL CONCERN? OFTEN IT IS NOT, AND IT CAN BE SAFELY OVERLOOKED. BUT IF IT IS A MATTER OF CONCERN, MOVE TO THE SECOND C, *CONFER.* A LOW-KEY CONFERENCE OFTEN RESOLVES A SITUATION. IF CONFERRING DOES NOT WORK, MOVE TO THE THIRD C, *CONSULT.* A MORE FORMAL CONSULTATION IS IN ORDER. IF THE SITUATION PERSISTS, THEN THE FINAL C, *CONFRONT,* IS APPROPRIATE. THIS FINAL C REQUIRES A DIRECT, NO-NONSENSE, THIS-IS-HOW-IT-IS APPROACH. BUT REMEMBER TO BEGIN WITH THE LESS DEMANDING C'S FIRST. RESOLVE SITUATIONS AT THE LOWEST POSSIBLE LEVEL OF CONFLICT. THIS SAVES A LOT OF ENERGY.

* Purkey, W.W. (1970). *Self-concept and school achievement.* Englewood Cliffs, NJ: Prentice-Hall, Inc.

Activity 1.16
Conflict Management Strategies

Level:

Grades 3 to 8

Purpose:

To explore 10 different ways to manage or solve a conflict with another individual.

Materials:

Ten slips of paper each with one of the conflict management strategies listed below and defined.

Activity I:

You might say: *We are going to explore 10 ways in which we can face a conflict. These 10 ways are called conflict management strategies or plans.* Describe each of the 10 conflict management strategies below, using examples appropriately to the age level of the group with which you are working.

Conflict Management Strategies

1. **Sharing**—the individuals decide to share for the benefit of both.
2. **Taking turns**—one individual goes first and the other second.
3. **Chance**—a technique such as flipping a coin is used to decide the outcome of a conflict.
4. **Humor**—the angry feelings associated with conflict are diffused in some humorous and constructive way.
5. **Distracting**—calling attention to something else as a way of diffusing the conflict.
6. **Apologizing**—saying you are sorry without necessarily saying you are wrong
7. **Soliciting Intervention**—seeking consultation or help when the issue is too complex or heavy to handle.
8. **Postponing**—individuals agree to wait for a more appropriate time to handle the situation.
9. **Abandoning**—moving away from a situation which cannot be dealt with.
10. **Negotiating and Compromising**—individuals talk about their position in the conflict and discuss what might be done about it. Both parties may give up something to resolve the conflict.

Activity II:

Divide the class into 10 groups. Give each group one of the conflict management strategies. Ask the groups to devise a short skit which has a conflict that is solved by the strategy on their slips of paper. Then ask the groups to come up front and perform their skit while the rest of the groups try to guess which strategy they were depicting. (You may want to video the skits and then play them back to facilitate the guessing.)

Closure:

Do a go-around letting each person complete the statement: *I learned or relearned today that_____.*

Activity 1.17

Freeze, Face, Fight, or Flight

Level: Grades 3 to 12

Purpose: To define conflict and explore conflict styles.

Materials: Paper, crayons, or markers.

Activity: Begin by asking for two volunteers to come to the front of the group and to sit back to back. Ask the group to describe a common disagreement that students their age may have. Then, have the volunteers role play the argument as you tie them together with yarn or string. Then, say: *People tend to think that being in conflict with another is like a tug-of-war, but it really is more like being tied together. The two in conflict now have a common problem which has to be dealt with.*

Ask: *How can the two in conflict be "untied?"* As the group gives their answers, untie the volunteers if the answer demonstrates assessing the conflict and/or working toward management or a resolution of the problem.

Next, explain the conflict style model as shown on the next page: "Freeze, Face, Fight, or Flight." Emphasize that these conflict responses are partly physiological and that all animals including the human animal responds in one of the four ways. Use an example of an animal being confronted by a predator and how it might react in each of the four ways.

Then, ask the students to remember some conflicts they have recently been in. Ask them to remember how they reacted. Then have the students imagine an animal that best describes how they themselves react to conflict, i.e., a turtle which withdraws its head into its shell when confronted with conflict (flight). Now, ask the students to draw that animal. (The students may want to draw an animal which is a combination of two animals if they react in two different ways. Give an example of your own "conflict style animal" before they begin to draw theirs.)

Divide the students into groups of 5 or 6 and ask them to share their drawings and an example of a conflict in which they acted like the animal they drew.

Closure: You might say: *We all deal with conflict in different ways. In most conflict situations with friends and family, facing the conflict and finding a reasonable solution tends to be the best way to deal with a problem.*

Joe Wittmer, Ph.D. and Diane W. Thompson, M.Ed.

Conflict Styles*

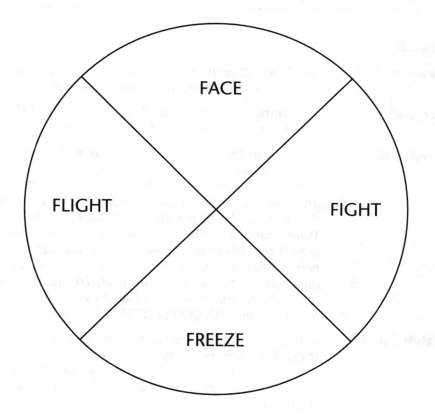

FACE—ASSESSING THE ISSUE(S) IN CONFLICT AND WORKING TOWARD MANAGEMENT OR RESOLUTION

FIGHT—ENGAGING IN CONFRONTATION AND WIN/LOSE BEHAVIORS LEADING TO SELF DEFENSIVENESS

FREEZE—SUCCUMBING TO FEARFUL AND ANXIOUS EMOTIONS WHICH PRODUCE A FROZEN OR SUBMISSIVE RESPONSE

FLIGHT—CHOOSING TO IGNORE OR AVOID CONFLICT THROUGH WITHDRAWAL OR DISTRACTING BEHAVIORS

*Adapted from: Hart, L. (1981). *Learning from conflict.* Boston: Addison Wesley.

Activity 1.18

Human Bingo

Level:	Grades 3 to 12
Purpose:	To allow students to get to know one another better and to develop better oral and written communication.
Materials:	Two handouts: "Human Bingo" and "Find the Person Who" along with small slips of paper in a hat numbering from 1 to 25.
Activity I:	You might begin by saying: *Today we're going to do a fun activity that will help us get to know each other better. We may find out some unique bits of information about each other.* Next, distribute the "Find a Person Who" and the "Human Bingo" handouts. *You are to walk around the room and find people who fit the qualifications of the items on your "Find a Person Who" handout. When you find a person who fits a particular item, have that person sign his or her name in any square. Put the number of the item that person "fits" in the square with the signature. You may not use any person or question more than once. Fill in all 16 squares and then sit down. I'll call time in 5 minutes and then we'll play BINGO! Any questions? Begin finding people to fill up your BINGO BOARD!*
Activity II:	When everyone is seated tell them: *I am going to draw numbers from a hat. If I call out a number that is on your Bingo chart, mark an "X" in that number square. When you get 4 in a row horizontally, vertically, or diagonally, call out BINGO!* Finish game and award winner a small prize (pack of life savers, stickers).
Closure:	Say: *We've learned a little more about each other today. Would anyone like to share what they learned about someone else? Perhaps share something you found out today that you have in common with another in this group.* (Let the students answer.)
	We've learned today through playing "Human Bingo" that we have some things in common and finding things in common can build good relationships and help you to make new friends.

Joe Wittmer, Ph.D. and Diane W. Thompson, M.Ed.

Find a Person

Directions:

1. Find a person who meets the qualifications of each item below.
2. Have that person sign (neatly) your card in any square.
3. Write the question number in same square as name.
4. You cannot use any person or any question number more than once.

Find a person who...

1. Has a last name that begins with the same letter as your last name.
2. Was born in the same month and year as you.
3. Likes to talk on the phone at least an hour every night.
4. Likes the same music group as you.
5. Has seen the movie "Back to the Future."
6. Has played on an organized athletic team in a league.
7. Has a friend who is famous.
8. Lives in the same neighborhood.
9. Likes Physical Education.
10. Has had breakfast at McDonald's this week.
11. Thinks school attendance should be voluntary after the fifth grade.
12. Was born in Florida.
13. Shares your favorite food.
14. Has never smoked a cigarette.
15. Lives in a two-story house.
16. Lives in an apartment.
17. Speaks a foreign language.
18. Has been to the beach in the last two weeks.
19. Uses the same brand of toothpaste as you.
20. Has a mountain bike.
21. Watches TV at least two hours a day.
22. Has gone water skiing.
23. Has the same favorite TV show as you.
24. Has the same hobby as you.
25. Likes Cherry Coke.

Human Bingo!

Joe Wittmer, Ph.D. and Diane W. Thompson, M.Ed.

SECTION II
CROSS-CULTURAL AWARENESS AND COMMUNICATION

This section contains several large group activities that will assist K-12 students in gaining self-awareness concerning their feelings and perceptions regarding those who are culturally different from them. In addition, the activities were developed so the students would learn skills that aid in their communication with those who are different.

Our awareness and willingness to understand others is a major key to effective communication with the culturally different. It is important that students learn to be aware of others' thoughts and feelings, regardless of their race, creed, gender, or cultural background. Effective facilitative communicators are aware of other persons' frames of reference and their views of the world regardless of their cultural background.

Students should understand that they can learn skills that will assist them in understanding how others view their worlds and react to them, as opposed to telling them how they should react and behave toward their own worlds! In introducing this section you might say: *Others' world views may be very different from yours, but they are based on their perceptions—which are their realities. And, their reality determines how they feel, think, and behave. The quality of the relationship between you and a culturally different person may be the most important ingredient for effective communication. Relationships are enhanced if we are aware of the feelings we have towards those different from us. In addition, if we want to be effective communicators with such individuals, we need to work hard at changing any negative attitudes we may have about a particular cultural group or race. We need to look outside ourselves, step back, and take a hard look at ourselves! What do you see when you look in the mirror? A person who is open or biased? Someone who believes that those who are culturally different need to be "taken care" of?* Students should understand that if they are an Anglo American, for example, they may be viewed as a representative of a general society which has oppressed many culturally different groups.

It is important that students of all ages realize that self-aware individuals avoid a condescending attitude and do not patronize culturally different persons. To patronize implies the belief that we hold a superior position to them—we come across to them as being "better" than they. And, members of other cultural groups view this as disrespectful. Relatedly, some Anglo Americans seem to have a characteristic that could best be described as "assumed similarity." That is, they assume that people either ought to be like them or want to be like them!

Psychologists indicate that we tend to give up our assumptions only after we have been confronted by data that shows our assumptions are wrong. We tend to search for evidence to support biased assumptions. Unfortunately, the reverse is seldom true. We do not often look for things to disprove erroneous assumptions. Self-awareness is the key to changing the invalid assumptions we hold about other groups. Several activities in this section address the negative assumptions commonly held regarding other cultural groups.

There are many skills needed to be an effective multi-racial, multi-ethnic communicator. Communicating with those different from us must entail more than techniques or philosophy. We, as individual human beings, are the major ingredient. Our own philosophy of life, and self-awareness combined with skills and knowledge of the culture, yield the most effective communication. Several such skills are inherent in various activities included in this section.

Some Basic Guidelines and Assumptions

The following guidelines are basic to communicating effectively with individuals from culturally different groups and should be strongly emphasized to students prior to having them participate in any activities given in this section:

1. Individual rather than mass methods and techniques of communicating with individuals are important regardless of the cultural group.

2. The individual, not the cultural group, should be the unit of consideration. The individual is a person primarily, and an African American or Hispanic American, for example, secondarily.

And finally, emphasize to students that in America we are rapidly becoming a multi-ethnic society. And, that all Americans must learn to communicate more effectively with one another, regardless of cultural or racial backgrounds. It is obvious that there are many communication barriers and these need to be addressed if our country is to survive its own diversity. To move forward, we must respect one another's uniqueness, our sameness, and our differences; we cannot insist on being a "melting pot" society. The writers believe that among other things, accurate information and knowledge are essential and necessary as a foundation for communicating effectively with culturally distinct persons. However, self-awareness, awareness of others, being sensitive, and learning some communication skills that "work" may be the most important. That is the focus of this section.

Activity 2.1

Becoming a Member of Another Culture: A Fantasy

Level:	Grades 6 to 12
Purpose:	For students to learn what it would be like to suddenly find themselves as members of another culture.
Materials:	None.
Activity:	Ask the students to relax and to close their eyes. (You may wish to conduct a brief relaxation activity before beginning.) Read the following fantasy aloud, pausing where necessary and deemed appropriate:

The Fantasy

You're feeling relaxed now; you're very calm; it's in the middle of the week, just prior to bed time. You find yourself sitting in your comfortable chair very relaxed. Your eyes are closing.... You are tired, very tired, and decide to go to bed. You enter a very restful sleep, a very restful sleep. It's just one of those nights when you feel very good, very sleepy, very restful. (Pause 15 seconds.) Now, visualize yourself awakening the next morning. You see yourself entering your bathroom. Take a careful look in the mirror; you see there's been a rather startling transformation during the night.... You woke up as a member of another culture with physical characteristics typical of those from that culture.... You went to bed as a member of one culture and you woke up a member of another! (Pause.) *How does it feel?* (Pause.) *What are your thoughts as you look at yourself in the mirror?* (Pause.) *Now, you find yourself walking outside and meeting your best friend. How does your friend react?* (Pause.) *Now, visualize yourself walking across the campus. How do people react to you? You meet your favorite teacher—what happens? How do you feel? What is the overall reaction towards you?* (Pause.) *OK. Open your eyes now.*

Now, place the students into groups of 5 or 6 and request that they take turns sharing their respective fantasies. Suggest that they use facilitative responses—tuning in to feelings, clarifying/summarizing, and/or open-ended questions (what, how, when or where)—during their discussion with one another. Specifically, request that they not "interpret" another's fantasy. However, self-interpretation may be appropriate.

Closure:	Lead a discussion with the entire class for the purpose of bringing out the various themes found in the students' fantasies and their specific reactions to suddenly being a member of a different culture.

Activity 2.2

Dear Abby and the Cool Seat

Level:	Grades 7 to 12
Purpose:	This exercise permits a greater awareness of the problems that those "different" from us are experiencing and provides the opportunity to give timely advice when preceded by a "tuning in to others' feelings" oriented response.
Materials:	"Dear Abby" statements (pre-written or written directly preceding the activity by the participants) and a large sign stating "Cool Seat."
Activity:	Place the participants in small, culturally homogeneous groups (4 or 5) and ask them to write Dear Abby about current problems they are facing relating to their respective racial or cultural backgrounds, (i.e., communication with the majority culture, etc.). Request that they keep the problem statements short (6 or 7 lines) and that they not personally refer to anyone by name.

The Dear Abby procedure is a fish bowl-type discussion activity to be used with large groups. After the problems are written (they might also be written by individual participants), develop a horseshoe-type circle up front, with the opening toward the larger group, and call for 6 volunteers, i.e., six Anglos, three males and three females, to enter into the "fish bowl" to play the part of Dear Abby to give "timely advice" to the African American, Asian American, Hispanic American, and/or other culturally distinct participants who have written Dear Abby. That is, they are to solve the participants' problems written by those different from them. The horseshoe shape permits an empty chair at its opening which is termed the cool seat and is so designated by a large, printed sign on the back of the chair. Fishbowl members (i.e., the six Anglos) are in the hot seats at this time; they are the problem solvers! Any member from the audience (not in the fish bowl) may join the fishbowl only by standing behind the cool seat chair. You, or someone of your choice, should serve as facilitator in the fishbowl and begin the process by giving one of the Anglo participants a problem, i.e., one that a Hispanic participant wrote to Dear Abby, who, in turn, as Dear Abby solves the Hispanic participant's problem. However, the persons playing Dear Abby should always state the feelings they think the writers are feeling (pleasant, unpleasant or both) to have written such a statement prior to giving the timely advice to the writers. Then, they indicate how a person who is feeling that way usually behaves. That is, prior to giving timely advice to the writer of the problem, members in the "hot seats" are asked to tune in to the feelings of each writer and indicate what actions such feelings usually cause-"What would the writer most likely be feeling?" Then, "What behavior(s) would such a feeling most likely cause?" Then they follow with timely advice in a "Dear Abby" manner.

This almost always creates a lively discussion and many people from the outside group may line up behind the cool seat to voice their views. However, they get only 30 seconds in the "cool seat" and are requested not to use personal names, to stay with the topic, and so forth. After the Anglo "hot seat" participants solve the Hispanic participants' problems (about one half hour), call up 6 Hispanic volunteers to enter the fishbowl and, in turn, solve the problems written to Dear Abby by Anglo/Black/Asian American participants, and others. Again, advice should be preceded by tuning in to feeling statements followed by a statement concerning the behavior most likely resulting from such feelings. Because of the obvious emotions and tension brought about by this activity, be prepared to facilitate and demonstrate by using high facilitative counseling type responses.

Note: Having the problems written in advance and edited by you tends to work best for this type activity.

Closure: Lead a large group discussion regarding what was learned from the activity.

A Variation: Have the males and females write to Dear Abby and in turn solve one another's problems, tuning in to feelings, resulting behavior, and so forth with the different genders (6 or 8 participants) taking turns in the "hotseat" solving the others' gender-related problems.

Activity 2.3

Me as Communicator:
With Those Different and Those Similar

Level:

Grades 7 to 12

Purpose:

To assist students in self-awareness as well as awareness of others who may be similar and/or different from them.

Materials:

Have a copy of "Me As Communicator" available for each participant.

Activity:

Ask the students to complete the "Me as Communicator" scale by placing an "A" and a "D" on the appropriate line for each set of the two opposing descriptive characteristics. Ask them to respond as honestly as possible so as to increase their self-awareness. They should place an "A" (Actual) ABOVE the line indicating "where you actually are as a communicator" and a "D" (Desired) Below the line to indicate "where you would like to be as a communicator." *Respond to each set of opposing words twice, once as you actually are and once as how you would like to be. For example, for the first set of words, if you see yourself a little more negative than the average person, you would place an "A" ABOVE the line somewhere around 5 or 6. However, if you desire to be "very positive" you would place a "D" BELOW the line somewhere around 1 or 2. After you've finished, be prepared to share it with others.* Allow ten minutes to complete the survey. Then, divide the participants into small groups of 5 or 6 each. Each group should elect a leader (or you might appoint them) to lead a group discussion on the survey "Me as a Communicator." Set the following ground rules for each group:

1. Share your ideas, thoughts, and feelings.
2. Listen to each other's ideas, thoughts, and feelings without interruption, judgment, untimely advice giving, interpretation, or evaluation.
3. Anyone can pass at any time (i.e., not respond or share).

Closure:

Bring the small groups back into a discussion with the larger group. Some questions might be:

1. *What did you learn about yourself today as a communicator?*
2. *How will what you learned affect your ability to communicate more effectively with those similar and those different from you?*

Joe Wittmer, Ph.D. and Diane W. Thompson, M.Ed.

Me As A Communicator

(Actual "A" and Desired "D")

1   2   3   4   5   6   7

positive	negative
honest	dishonest
introverted	extroverted
fluent	diffluent
friendly	unfriendly
loud	quiet
open	closed
tense	relaxed
intellectual	nonintellectual
static	changeable
calm	excitable
empathic	unempathic
listener	non-listener
conservative	liberal
hard	soft
unbiased	biased
humorous	serious
soft	loud
prejudiced	non-prejudicial
shallow	deep
strong	weak
kind	unkind
accepting	nonaccepting
optimistic	pessimistic
ferocious	peaceful

Activity 2.4

Developing an Appreciation for Cultural Differences I*

(Session 1 of 6)

Introduction to the Six Sessions:

During the elementary school years, students move from being spontaneous and magical to becoming more concrete and absolute. With this in mind, the following six-session group guidance unit was designed to enhance an understanding of same and different. Each of the six sessions was planned to last approximately 20 to 30 minutes, an appropriate attention span expectation for elementary school students, and were designed for groups of approximately 25 to 30 students.

Level: Grades K to 5

Purpose: The purpose of the first large group guidance session is to provide a concrete, simple experience of same and different in order to introduce the ideas in a manner that will best encourage the students to want to continue.

Materials: The materials needed for this session are three clear, glass containers, some flour, table salt, yellow corn meal, chalkboard or flip chart, chalk and/or magic markers.

Activity: Begin this first session by agreeing on the guidelines for speaking and listening. We suggest simple guidelines stated in the positive:

1. *We listen to and respect one another's thoughts, ideas, and feelings.*

2. *We share, when comfortable, our own ideas, thoughts and feelings*

3. *Anyone can pass a turn if they wish (i.e., you will not be forced to participate).*

Elementary school students appreciate knowing the rules by which they are expected to play. At the beginning of each subsequent session it is helpful if the counselor requests the students to remind one another of the guidelines for behavior as noted above.

Next, place the three glass containers on a table. Put a substantial amount of flour in the first, table salt in the second, and yellow corn meal in the third. Do not tell the students the contents of the containers.

*Adapted from Faubert, M., Locke, D.C., & McLeod, P.W. (1993). The counselor's role in teaching students to value cultural diversity;. in Wittmer, J. (1993). *Managing your school counseling program: K-12 developmental strategies*. Minneapolis, MN: Educational Media Corporation.

We suggest you say something like this to the students: *Tell me how the substance in the first bowl looks. If I could not see it, how would you describe it to me?* (Repeat this activity for bowls two and three.)

Place the words same and different on a chalkboard or a flip chart. Ask the students how the contents of the bowls are the same and how they are different. Write the descriptive words given to you by the students on the board or flip chart in the corresponding column under the words same or different.

It is acceptable if some of the words are not in the reading vocabulary of the students. They are in their speaking vocabulary; therefore, it is appropriate to place them in their visual range. Early elementary school students might give some magical answers. Older elementary school students will probably provide more concrete descriptions of the bowls' contents.

Ask the students to come forward in turn to place their hands in each of the bowls and to feel the contents. Have them describe how the contents of the bowls feel; how they feel the same and how they feel different from one another. Add their responses to the corresponding columns marked same and different.

Closure: Summarize with the students how the substances in the three bowls are the same and how they are different. Ask the students what other things that they know about are the same or different. Suggest to the students that they think of things that are the same and things that are different during the following week.

Activity 2.5

Developing an Appreciation for Cultural Differences II

(Session 2 of 6)

Level: Grades K to 5

Purpose: The purpose of the second session is to furnish the students with something potentially creative, something "hands on" in order for them to talk about same and different comfortably during the following week.

Materials: The material needed for this session is enough plasticine (play putty or play dough) of different colors for each child to have approximately equal amounts.

Activity: Have the students report what they remember about the first session and facilitate the discussion so as to "link" or "pair" student's responses where possible. That is, tie their responses together. This brings about more comfort and cohesiveness on the part of the larger group. Encourage the students to share what things they have thought of during the week that were the same and that were different. At the end of the introduction, ask each student to tell, to re-state, or to clarify to one other student in the group what that student just shared. This helps increase their listening skills and will result in their "tuning in to" other students.

Give each student plasticine (play putty or play dough) of approximately the same amount but of different colors, if possible. Suggest to them that they shape it into something that they like. Encourage the students to verbally share with the group what they have made. In turn, ask the students to tell how what they have made is unique but yet the same from what at least one other student in the room has made.

Closure: Summarize or clarify to the students how they seemed to feel about sharing sameness and difference with one another. Where possible, reflect their feelings, thoughts, and ideas. Help the students to understand that everything is the same in some ways and yet different in other ways. Finish this session by helping the students to understand that the sharing of sameness and difference can make them feel good and an important part of the group.

Joe Wittmer, Ph.D. and Diane W. Thompson, M.Ed.

Activity 2.6

Developing an Appreciation for Cultural Differences III

(Session 3 of 6)

Level: Grades K to 5

Purpose: To learn more about how sameness and difference influence how we view others.

Materials: The materials needed for this session are two telephones (play or real), two empty tables, and two additional chairs, one at each table.

Activity: Have the students review what they have learned about same and different to this point. And, during the discussion, have the students "tune in to" or "summarize the content" of what other students have shared. Introduce them to the idea that people are the same as one another and also different from one another. Ask them how people are the same as one another and how they are different from one another (gender, race, etc.).

Place one telephone on one of the tables (with an empty chair) and place another telephone on another table (a short distance away). Tell the students that in this activity they are going to pretend that a new boy or a new girl of a different culture or race from themselves is in their classroom for the first time. Ask them to pretend that it is after school and they are calling one of their best friends (on the telephone) to tell him or her about this pretend new classmate of theirs.

Have one student pretend to be the caller and another student pretend to be the friend called. After five or six pairs of students have had a turn, process and facilitate the content of the conversations. Encourage the students to talk about the kinds of things that they said about the new classmate that was "different" yet the "same" as they themselves are.

Closure: Summarize how the sameness or difference of the new classmate might influence how they described the new person to their friend.

Activity 2.7

Developing an Appreciation for Cultural Differences IV

(Session 4 of 6)

Level: Grades K to 5

Purpose: To share descriptions of themselves with others so as to learn more about how they are the same and/or different from others.

Materials: No special materials are needed for this session.

Review briefly what the students remember of the three previous sessions.

For this fourth week's activity, the students will concentrate more directly on themselves. Ask each student to share three adjectives (descriptions) about themselves. For example, "I am tall; I am Afro-American; I'm a girl; I like to read; I have a big sister." After each student has spoken, have the students pair up (by different culture, race, etc. where possible) and to tell each other one thing that they heard that is the same as they and one thing they heard that is different from that person with whom they are paired. Then, ask the students to share with the rest of the class some of the unique aspects they learned about their partner that is different from themselves.

Closure: Summarize by reflecting to the students how they feel about having some things about themselves that are the same as other students and some things that are different from other students. Provide a supportive environment so that the students will leave the session feeling good about being like (the same as) other students while also feeling good about being different from others as the case may be.

Joe Wittmer, Ph.D. and Diane W. Thompson, M.Ed.

Activity 2.8

Developing an Appreciation for Cultural Differences V

(Session 5 of 6)

Level:

Grades K to 5

Purpose:

To assist students in the skills of "tuning in to" others who are different.

Materials:

No special materials are needed for this session.

Activity:

First, review briefly what the students remember about the previous four sessions. You may wish to review the guidelines previously established.

Reflect to the students a positive, or pleasant feeling that they, as a group seem to have in relation to their remembrances. Be specific; it will be helpful if counselors name the students about whom they are speaking (i.e., "Joe, you felt encouraged to learn....") Encourage the students to talk about times when they were with people that were the same as they or were different from themselves. Stimulate the students to talk about how they get along with other students whom they see as the same and other students whom they see as different in class, at the mall, on the playground, or whatever. Again, facilitate the discussion by having students "tune in to" one another (i.e., to clarify another students thoughts ideas and/or feelings).

Have the students tell aloud (or to write on paper) how they are going to commit to work to appreciate those students whom they see as different from themselves and their friends and to give one or two things (concrete examples) they will personally do during the next month; sort of a personal contract to carry out their commitment. They may resolve to listen better or more closely to a student whom they perceive as different; to provide a warm welcome to a student whom they perceive as different into a game that they may be playing with their friends; or invite a student whom they perceive as different into a task that they have to perform in a group in the classroom, and so forth.

Closure:

Summarize or clarify how "tuning in to" another person who is different will make themselves, and the student who is different, also feel better.

Activity 2.9

Developing an Appreciation for Cultural Differences VI

(Session 6 of 6)

Level:	Grades K to 5
Purpose:	To further assist students to realize that individuals are the same yet different and to understand that there is strength in a diverse society.
Materials:	No special materials are needed for this final session.
Activity:	Begin with a discussion on what they remember from the previous five sessions. Then, tell the students that this is the last time they will be discussing this unit for now but you may, from time to time, focus on sameness and differences throughout the rest of the school year. Process their feelings about what they have learned about sameness and difference. Use the student's own stories to summarize what they have learned and have them rephrase, repeat, or restate what other students have learned. Stimulate them to provide examples of things they can think of that are the same and different (e.g., trees are the same and different; houses are the same and different; cars are the same and different and, most importantly, people are the same and yet different). Lead a discussion on the latter.
Closure:	Encourage the students to talk about how people are the same but different. What does this mean to them? Help them to understand that sameness and difference are part of life, that it is not only acceptable, but desirable. And finally, help them to appreciate that things and people are the same as one another and also different from one another; and that in our diversity, we have strength as a society.
Conclusion to the Six Sessions:	As the designers of personal computers are successful in producing a user friendly instrument by applying human development attributes, counselors of elementary school students can be successful in developing an appreciation of same and difference among themselves if they keep the developmental tasks of students in mind when preparing their large group guidance sessions. Counselors have a plethora of data to support the notion that it is vitally important to teach students to value diversity and differences—that the future of our society depends on it!
	As noted, elementary school students can be spontaneous, magical, concrete, and absolute. When these attributes of elementary school students are taken into consideration, successfully interventions can be designed to develop an appreciation for same and difference. Effective counselors use the lived experiences that the students share during the planned sessions as the fabric, the raw material and substance for teaching awareness, respect, and appreciation for same and different.

Joe Wittmer, Ph.D. and Diane W. Thompson, M.Ed.

Activity 2.10

Pick Your Corner: Taking a Stand

Level:	Grades 9 to 12
Purpose:	To encourage students to "take a stand" regarding their feelings, thoughts, and ideas on some difficult culturally related topics. This activity will also stimulate communication on important issues, force clarification of positions, and increase understanding of other's points of view.
Materials:	Paper and pencils
Activity I:	Designate one corner of the room (use large print) as the "Strongly Disagree" section, another as the "Strongly Agree" section, a third as the "Disagree" section, and a fourth as the "Agree" section. The center of the room might be designated as "Uncertain." Then, ask all participants to stand. Next, make a statement (just one) such as: *Minorities are getting too many breaks in America today*; or, *We should push segregation not integration*; or, *Affirmative Action is not working*; or *Regardless of culture, we're all more similar than different*; or *No culturally distinct group should have its own designated month, i.e. Black History Month.* Give the participants a brief time to think about the options given in the different "corners" of the room. Then, request that each walk to the corner that best matches their personal opinions/feelings about the statement. You might say: *Go where you really want to go, not to where your friends go!*

Allow time for the participants (maybe in groups of five if a large group chooses one specific corner) in each corner to discuss among themselves their reasons for choosing the particular corner. They should make a brief list of the reasons that led them to be there. Then, hold a general discussion as members listen to the statements from each of the different corners. You might bring a few from various groups into a "fishbowl" circle, perhaps to debate the issue or to try and convince the "Uncertain" group to pick a corner. In addition, after hearing from a particular "corner" give participants an opportunity to switch corners if they so desire.

Activity II:	Reassemble the entire class/group, have them stand, read the statement again, and ask the participants to go to the corner their parents (teachers, African-Americans, or others) might choose. Again, allow time for discussion among those who select a particular corner and follow the procedures given above.

Additional (Non-culturally related) topics for "Pick Your Corner"

1. Abortion should be legalized and available to everyone without restrictions.
2. Fidelity between partners with respect to sex is something one should not ask for.
3. Living on welfare should be made unattractive since a lot of people are born lazy.
4. Smoking should be banned from the streets, all public buildings and public transport altogether.
5. Nuclear armaments and nuclear power plants are a form of national suicide.
6. Capital punishment for certain crimes is not only necessary, it is desirable.
7. All political systems based on religious beliefs are dangerous.
8. Women can be good managers and provide leadership (including religious leadership) as well as men.
9. Married women should not work outside the house but should be at home to take care of the family.
10. Marijuana should be legalized.

Closure: It is important to process this activity in a final de-briefing of "Pick-Your-Corner." Let the students know that you appreciate their taking a "stand" on these important issues.

Joe Wittmer, Ph.D. and Diane W. Thompson, M.Ed.

Activity 2.11

Asian/Pacific Islanders and Western Values: A Comparison

Level: Grades 5 to 12

Purpose: To give students the opportunity to compare their personal values with those of Asian/Pacific Islanders.

Materials: A copy of the "Asian and Western Values" handout for each participant.

Activity: Give each student a copy of the "Asian and Western Values" handout, divide the participants into groups of 5 or 6, appoint a leader for each group, and request that they share their feelings, thoughts, and ideas regarding the handout. Remind them to tune into one another's feelings, thoughts, and ideas, and that anyone may pass a turn. Suggest to the small group leaders that they lead the discussion and then be prepared to return to the larger group prepared to discuss the following:

1. The difference in values between the Asian/Pacific Islanders and Western cultures as given in the handout.

2. How might these differences impede communication between an Asian/Pacific Islander and an Anglo American, or any other non-Asian?

3. Select the nonverbal opposites found in the two lists and indicate how they might affect your communication with an Asian American. Or, if Asian, with an Anglo.

Closure: Lead a final discussion on what they learned today and how it personally affected them.

Some Questions to Ponder

1. What are some differences in values between the Asian/Pacific Islanders and Western cultures as given in the handout?

2. How might these differences impede communication between an Asian/Pacific Islander and an Anglo American, or any other non-Asian?

3. Select the nonverbal opposites found in the two lists and indicate how they might affect your communication with an Asian American. Or, if Asian, with an Anglo.

Asian and Western Values

Look carefully at the two opposing lists below and answer the questions that follow. Be prepared to share your reactions with others.

Asian	Western
We live in time.	You live in space.
We are always at rest.	You are always on the move.
We are passive.	You are aggressive.
We like to contemplate.	You like to act.
We accept the world as it is.	You try to change it according to your blue print.
We live in peace with nature.	You try to impose your will on her.
Religion is our first love.	Technology is your passion.
We delight to think about the meaning of life.	You delight in physics.
We believe in freedom of silence.	You believe in freedom of speech.
We lapse into meditation.	You strive for articulation.
We marry first, then love.	You love first, then marry.
Our marriage is the beginning of a love affair.	Your marriage is the happy end of a romance.
It is an indissoluble bond.	It is a contract.
Our love is mute.	Your love is vocal.
We try to conceal it from the world.	You delight in showing it to others.
Self-denial is a secret to our survival.	Self-assertiveness is the key to your success.
We are taught from the cradle to want less and less.	You are urged every day to want more and more.
We glorify austerity and renunciation.	You emphasize gracious living and enjoyment.
Poverty is a badge of spiritual elevation.	It is to you a sign of degradation.
In the sunset years of life we renounce the world and prepare for the hereafter.	You retire to enjoy the fruits of your labor.

(Anonymous)

Activity 2.12

Communication Between the Races/Cultures

Level:

Grades 6 to 12

Purpose:

This is an exercise aimed at facilitating communication between two different races or cultures and to heighten awareness of stereotypes/prejudices.

Materials:

None.

Activity:

From among all the class/group members, form two circles, one circle within another, i.e., African-Americans might sit in the inside circle while all non-Blacks sit on the outside. For the first ten minutes encourage the Blacks to talk about communication problems with Anglos (in general), venting their unpleasant and pleasant feelings (no personal names). The outer circle of non-Blacks observes but does not participate in the discussion. After about ten minutes, the circles are reversed, with the non-Blacks on the inside responding to the same task (problems in communication with Blacks, in general). (Any cultural group can take their turn in the "fishbowl," i.e., Hispanic Americans, Asian/Pacific Islanders, and/or others).

Closure:

Next, have both groups together discuss how they felt about the activity and what they learned from it. Additional questions to each group might be posed by group members or you.

Note: Facilitative responses should be used.

A Variation:

Have the females sit in the inside circle and pretend they are males. They talk about how it feels to be "male" and what they like and dislike about it. They might also talk about how they see females, or talk about: "Things I like and dislike about being a man or woman," or "Things that I would like to change in our society in terms of being masculine or feminine." Each group might be encouraged to talk about the biggest problem of the opposite sex.

Another variation is to have the males write statements about what it feels like to be a male and some of their likes and dislikes. The statements are then given to the circle of females, who read them and respond. For example, "My girlfriend makes me feel cheap when I can't afford to take her to certain places;" or "Why do guys always have to be the ones to set up a date?" or, "I like a girl, but she doesn't like me," and so forth.

Activity 2.13

Cultural Awareness

Level: Grades 5 to 12

Purpose: To assist students in becoming more aware of how their own culture has helped or hindered in their current attitudes toward those who are different.

Materials: Have copies of the questions (found below) available for each participant.

Activity: Ask the students to respond to the following questions (briefly) in writing and to prepare responses to share with others.

1. When you hear the term culturally different, what group comes to mind first? Describe the participants of this culture in regard to their physical features, language, behaviors, attitudes, and lifestyles.

   The group _____

   Their personal characteristics _____

   _____

2. Think of the significant people in your life when you were a child (e.g., relatives, friends, or teachers). What do you remember about their attitudes toward other ethnic minority groups, i.e., African, Hispanic, Native, and/or Asian Americans? What can you hear them saying to you? What did you overhear that was intended for someone else's ears? What messages did you learn about these four groups from?

   a. Your parents or other relatives. _____

   _____

   b. The movies you've seen. TV. _____

   _____

   c. What messages do you give to others about these groups? ____

   _____

3. Think of the cultural group to which you belong. When did you first become aware, and how did you learn that you were a member of a group that was different from other groups? What did you learn about your cultural group in relation to other cultural groups?

Joe Wittmer, Ph.D. and Diane W. Thompson, M.Ed.

Allow at least 10 minutes for the students to complete their responses to the above. Then, divide the class members into small groups of 5 or 6 for the purpose of discussing the responses to the three questions posed above. Appoint a leader for each group and ask that person to lead the discussion based on the following open-ended questions:

1. What have you learned, or relearned, about yourself by responding to the questions regarding different groups?

2. What are you most aware of now about yourself or the groups?

3. What struck you most about this activity?

4. What did you learn about yourself that surprised you?

5. What did you learn about yourself that has the strongest implications for multicultural communication?

6. What experiences or events did you recall that have had the greatest impact on your present attitudes and feelings toward culturally distinct persons?

7. Now that you have brought many of these feelings to your awareness, what, if anything, would you like to change and/or do?

Closure: Bring the small groups back into the larger group and ask the small group leaders to share the sentiments of, and salient points made, by their particular small group regarding this activity.

Activity 2.14

Appreciating Diversity I*

(Session 1 of 4)

Level: Middle School—Grades 6 to 8

Introduction to the Four Sessions:

During the middle school years, students move from being concrete and absolute to being able to think more abstractly. With this in mind, the following four large group sessions are designed for enhancing an understanding of same and different for middle school aged students. Each of these sessions is planned to last approximately 30 to 40 minutes, an appropriate attention span expectation for middle school students. The sessions are designed for classes of 20 or more students. If you are working with more or fewer students, you can modify the activity to the class size. We urge the classroom teacher to remain in the room during these sessions so as to better conduct follow-up activities concerning the material being presented.

Middle school students are very creative. They enjoy performing. Because they are physically active, they appreciate the opportunity to "do" as well as to think. The structures for concrete either/or thinking are well developed, and students of this age like to solve problems. From becoming overly logical and concrete, middle school students begin to consider new factors and change their minds. They are moving from being appropriately self-protective to being appropriately conformist.

Since middle school students are comfortable with guidelines for behavior that are applied to all in the same way, begin the first session by discussing and agreeing upon the policies to which the class will adhere during the sessions. Middle school students will appreciate having been part of the policy making and will help enforce equal adherence to the guidelines. The agreed upon guidelines can be posted. You can refer to them whenever it is appropriate. We suggest the guidelines be stated in the positive (i.e., "We listen to one another" as opposed to "We don't interrupt one another," and so forth.

Purpose: To assist students in understanding how they are similar and different from other students.

Materials: The materials needed for this first session are newsprint, magic markers, and masking tape.

*Adapted from Faubert, M., Locke, D.C., & McLeod, F.W. (1993). The counselor's role in teaching students to value cultural diversity; in Wittmer, J. (1993) *Managing your school counseling program: K-12 developmental strategies*. Minneapolis, MN: Educational Media Corporation.

Activity:

Give each student one piece of newsprint and one magic marker. Have each write at least five words to describe themselves on the newsprint under their names. When finished, have them tape their newsprint sheet on the classroom wall or chalkboard.

Observe with the students which words are repeated from person to person and which words are unique to all individual students. Reflect with the students that there are characteristics that some have in common and characteristics that are unique to them as individuals. Again, facilitate the discussion so as to have students "tune in to" one another's thoughts, ideas and/or feelings.

Encourage the students to explore what happens in the classroom when a student is perceived as different by the other students. Have them discuss concrete examples of when they saw students who were perceived as different being isolated, ignored, or censured. List the characteristics that rejected students might have. Encourage the students to provide concrete examples to express their feelings about rejection. Facilitate their feelings and stay on your toes; middle school students may say anything. Be prepared to use your best group counseling skills. Provide a lot of support; this can be a discordance producing activity. Dissonance is required for growth, but be prepared to handle it with reassurance, encouragement, and gentle facilitation.

Stimulate the students to think of solutions to the problems that arise as a result of some students being rejected or ridiculed by other students because they are thought of as different. Prompt the students to provide concrete examples of how they can include others who are different in their study, play groups, or trips to the mall. Students at this age like to solve problems. Help the students to see that the difficulties that result from issues of difference can be thought of as opportunities to solve problems.

Closure:

Assist the students in summarizing concretely some of the ideas and suggestions resulting from the session. Ask them to make statements revealing their understanding of what others in the class have said (i.e., "Bill, as you listened to Jane talk, what did you hear? Summarize what she said for the rest of us.") Emphasize that they are to think about what has transpired in the session for fifteen minutes each day between this session and the next session (one week hence).

Assignment:

Ask them to write their reflections in a personal journal each day and bring their reflections to the next session. Indicate that some may want to share their reflections with their classroom teacher during the week. You may wish to give each student a handout that specifically structures the writings of a daily reflection journal.

Activity 2.15

Appreciating Diversity II

(Session 2 of 4)

Level:	Grades 6 to 8
Purpose:	To assist students in understanding where being "different" could become a problem in their lives and in the lives of others.
Materials:	The materials needed for this second session are the written reflections that the students were assigned in the previous session. (A variation would be to place them into small groups to write their reflections at this time.)
Activity:	Have the students share what they remember from the previous discussion. Ask them to share some of their written reflections. Reflect and clarify back to them their feelings in an accepting manner. Collect their written reflections. Go over the reflections (anonymously) and discuss as appropriate.
	Then, discuss different places/times in the students' lives where difference might be a problem. Develop some concrete ideas around experiences in their neighborhoods, churches, classrooms, playgrounds, and so forth which involve differences of culture, economics, and life style—brain-storm. Keep the students on task and as concrete as possible. Include specific examples of solutions to the problems presented in the personal reflections.
	Tell the students that they are going to dramatize (conduct a skit in front of the group) an example of a difference where it has, or could become, a problem with students at your school. Divide the students into small heterogeneous groups and inform them that the skit they develop must include solutions to the problem they are illustrating. Let them know that they will present the skit in a later session. (You may want to present each group with a problem to solve in the skit instead of having them come up with their own.)
Closure:	Discuss how the ideas they shared might be used to plan a dramatization. Detail some examples with the students. Be specific.

 Joe Wittmer, Ph.D. and Diane W. Thompson, M.Ed.

Activity 2.16

Appreciating Diversity III

(Session 3 of 4)

Level:

Grades 6 to 8

Purpose:

To assist students in developing solutions to problems that might arise because of a diverse society.

Materials:

Materials needed for this session are a chalkboard or flip chart, chalk or magic markers.

Activity:

Review with the students and place on the chalkboard or flip chart some of the ideas that were generated in the previous session. Be concrete and specific. Accept all responses without comment. To use complimentary responses implies the permission to use critical reactions. Genuine acceptance of students' proposals without commentary will be interpreted as affirmation and result in more student openness.

Next, divide the members of the class into the groups of five each as you organized them last session and assign them to plan a dramatization illustrating a problem, or potential problem, caused by difference and/or diversity in school and its solution. Give the student groups ten minutes to decide on their topic (if not previously given). Encourage them to be creative—some will use rap, others a particular rock and roll song, posters, and so forth. Remind them that when they plan their topic they must include solutions to problems. Allow all but the last five minutes to plan their dramatizations. It is best to designate a leader for each group.

Closure:

Lead a discussion with the whole group on any concerns they might have regarding the forthcoming small group dramatizations. Remind them that they are responsible for any props needed for their specific dramatizations. Their respective skits should not exceed 4 to 5 minutes. Assist them in how they might practice their "skit" prior to next session.

Activity 2.17

Appreciating Diversity IV

(Session 4 of 4)

Level:	Grades 6 to 8
Purpose:	To help the students learn (and brainstorm) solutions (through dramatization) to possible problems that might arise because of differences and the diversity within our society.
Materials:	The students will need props for their dramatizations. It will be helpful if you persuade the students to take responsibility for acquiring their own props. Encouragement will help ensure effective dramatizations. Video taping the skits for replaying gives added impetus for the students to do the skits well.
Activity:	Have the different groups present their 4- to 5-minute dramatizations of solving problems resulting from issues of difference that they know about (or have heard about) at school. Influence the students to make their problem and its solution concrete and clear. Be affirming of the creative expressions of the students.
	Discuss each drama with the class as that specific skit is completed. Find meaningful ideas in the dramas. Be careful not to concentrate on one group more than another. Encourage the students to share their feelings. Reflect their feelings empathically and ask them to tune in to other students' feelings, concerns, and so forth. Stimulate the students to tell when they have felt different in similar situations as those dramatized in the respective skits.
	Have the student leaders in each of the groups summarize one or two things that would be helpful for the class to remember regarding their particular dramatic presentation. Have some students who were not in a particular dramatization share what they appreciated in a special way about others dramatizations. Make sure all dramatizations are affirmed by students, by yourself, and by the teacher (if present).
Closure:	Close this final session with a summary and expression of appreciation to the students for their contributions to the four guidance units.

Joe Wittmer, Ph.D. and Diane W. Thompson, M.Ed.

Activity 2.18

Inter-Racial Communication

Level: Grades 11 to 12

Purpose: This activity will assist different cultural and/or racial groups in understanding (and respecting) their similarities and differences.

Materials: Newsprint and felt tip pens.

Activity: **Note:** This exercise is written using African Americans and Hispanic Americans as an example only. Any homogenous groups can participate.

Begin this activity with homogenous groupings by race (6 to 7 African Americans at a table and 6 to 7 Hispanic Americans at separate tables). Each African American and Hispanic American group is given a piece of large newsprint and given the following assignment:

African Americans, what is it that Hispanic Americans do, in general, that causes the communication breakdown between the two races? (in general, at this school, etc.).

And then, turning to the Hispanic Americans:

Hispanics, what is it that African Americans do, in general, that is causing the communication breakdown between the races?

Next, ask each table to list (large enough to be viewed and read from across the room) eight to ten points (no personal names) on their newsprint using a large black felt tipped pen. When each table finishes their respective assignment, provide each with a new piece of newsprint and a red felt tipped pen and give the following (surprise) assignment:

What did the other groups write about you? List 5 or 6 points.

Then, after they've completed this second part of the assignment, bring the participants together into a heterogeneous circle (with their respective newsprint's) to a "new" group setting and facilitate the discussion. (Caution: Do not let this develop into an argumentative, judgmental, blaming type activity. Use the facilitative model of communication—open-ended questions, clarification, and tuning in to feelings responses).

Did the respective groups know (quite accurately) what the "other" group wrote about them? Usually we know what is causing our interpersonal communication problems with others; we simply have not discussed our differences in a facilitative manner with one another.

Closure: Lead a discussion with the entire class on what they learned about themselves and about others as a result of this activity.

Activity 2.20

Inter-Cultural Understanding (Via Poetry)

(May be adapted to two or more sessions)

Level:	Grades 5 to 12
Purpose:	To stimulate students' thinking regarding inter cultural communication through poetry.
Materials:	One copy of the five (5) poems for each participant.
Activity:	Divide the class into groups of 4 or 5 and appoint a leader to lead a discussion on the messages implied in these five poems. Indicate that the leaders will be reporting back to the entire class regarding their specific group's feelings/reaction to the five poems.
Variation:	Give each group only one poem and ask them to react and report back to the entire group.
Closure:	After each group leader has reported, bring the small groups back to the larger group and lead a discussion on the activity. Some example discussion questions might be:

1. *What personal meaning did the poems have for you?*
2. *What did you find most striking about these poems?*
3. *What implications do the poems have for inter cultural communication?*

The Five Poems

In Germany, the Nazis first came for the communists,
  and I didn't speak up because I wasn't a communist.

Then they came for the Jews,
  and I didn't speak up because I wasn't Jewish.

Then they came for the trade unionist,
  and I didn't speak up because I wasn't a trade unionist.

Then they came for the Catholics,
  and I didn't speak up because I was a Protestant.

Then they came for me,
  and by that time there was no one left to speak for me.

Rev. Martin Niemoeller
German Lutheran pastor

Joe Wittmer, Ph.D. and Diane W. Thompson, M.Ed.

Herein lies the tragedy of the age not that men are poor
   All men know something of poverty
Not that men are wicked
   Who is good?
Not that men are ignorant
   What is truth?
Nay, but that men know so little.

            W.E.B. Dubois

Six humans trapped by happenstance
   In bleak and bitter cold,
Each one possessed a stick of wood
   Or so the story is told.

Their dying fire in need of logs
   The first man held his back,
For of the faces around the fire
   He noticed one was Black.

The next man looking across the way
   Saw one not of his church
And couldn't bring himself to give
   His stick of birch.

The third one sat in tattered clothes
   He gave his coat a hitch.
Why should his log be put to use
   To warm the idle rich?

The rich man just sat back and thought
   Of the wealth he had in store
And how to keep what he had earned
   From the lazy, shiftless poor.

The Black man's face bespoke revenge
   As the fire passed from his sight.
For all he saw in his stick of wood
   Was a chance to spite the White.

The last man of this forlorn group
   Did naught except for gain.
Giving only to those who gave
   Was how he played the game.

Their logs held tight in death's still hands
   Was proof of human sin.
They didn't die from the cold without.
   They died from the cold within.

            Anonymous

Stranger

Stranger, do not come one step nearer.
  Do not reach out toward me, stranger.
We must not touch our hands
  to join your loneliness and mine.

Abide by the regulation:
  no man shall approach a man,
no man shall approach a woman,
  nor man, woman, nor woman, man.
Our life depends on it.

You wear a red scarf,
  I wear a blue cap.
There can be nothing between us.
If you ask me the time, I must turn my wrist.
If I ask you the way, you must point.

The rules hang from every lamppost
  above the basket of geraniums.
They are nailed into the telephone poles.
Though we scream to break the silence,
who would conjecture the universality
of his sorrow?
Who would confess at the street corner?

Stranger, at the time of fire,
  you will pass through the smoke to save me.
Stranger, at the time of flood,
  I will lift you from the water.
At the time of the invader,
  we will gather together.

Guard us from our intimacy
  now, as we stand adjacent on the
endless belt conveying us into the future
  which, like the ancients' heaven,
will justify the disaster of this hour.

Peter Goblen

Asian is Not Oriental

ASIAN
is not
Oriental
head bowed, submissive, industrious
model minority
hard working, studious
quiet

  ASIAN
  is not being
  Oriental,
  Lotus blossom, exotic passion flower
  inscrutable

    ASIAN
    is not talking
    Oriental,
    ahh so, ching chong china man
    no tickee, no washee

ORIENTAL
is a white man's word.
Oriental is jap, flip, chink, gook
it's "how" 'bout a back rub mama-San"
it's "you" people could teach them niggers
and Mexicans a thing or two
you're good people
none of that 'hollering' and protesting"

  Oriental is slanty eyes, glasses, and buck teeth
  Charlie Chan, Tokyo Rose,
  Madam Butterfly
  it's "a half hour after eating Chinese food
  you're hungry again"
  it's houseboys, gardeners, and laundry men

    Oriental is a fad; yin-yang, kung fu
    "say one of them funny words for me"
    Oriental is downcast eyes, china doll
    "they all look alike."
    Oriental is sneaky
    Oriental
    is a white man's word.

WE
are not Oriental.
we have heard the word all our lives
we have learned to be Oriental
we have learned to live it, speak it,
play the role,
and to survive in a white world
become the role.
The time has come
to look at who gave us the name.

Anonymous (1989)

Activity 2.20

The Slap in the Dark*

Level: Grades 9 to 12

Purpose: To facilitate a discussion by students regarding prejudice and stereotypes. This activity can be effectively used as the first exercise in a series on prejudice. You may wish to make the activity more locally relevant by changing the name of the city and the cultural identity of the individuals in the story.

Materials: None.

Activity: Students should be placed in small groups of 5 to 6 each. Appoint a discussion leader for each group. Then, introduce and explain the exercise. Students are told only that a story will be read aloud, once only, in four separate parts. Between each part allow five minutes for the individual groups to discuss some questions and to make a brief report. The final three questions should be discussed after returning to the large group session. Read the text slowly and clearly, and only once, beginning with the title:

A: The Slap in the Dark

In a New York subway train a small group of people, the only ones in this particular car, were seated: a poorly dressed Mexican-American man, his Mexican-American girlfriend, a uniformed military policeman, a white Anglo mother and her beautiful blond haired, twenty year-old daughter. There was a power failure and the lights went out. For half a minute, until the train reached the next stop, it was pitch dark. Apart from a few comments about the sudden darkness, two other sounds could be heard—a kiss and a hard slap! At the next stop the white girl reported that her purse had been stolen. One of the passengers asked a subway official to search all passengers in the car.

Now, give each group 5 minutes to discuss the following questions and to then make a brief report to the rest of the class concerning their answers to the following questions:

1. Exactly what happened?

2. Why do you think this is so—what are the reasons behind your interpretation?

*Adapted from Oomkes, F.R. & Thomas, R.H. (1992). *Developing cross-cultural communication.* Gower, Ardershot, England: Connaught Training Limited.

Now, read the following (only once):

B: This is what the mother thought: "What a great girl, this daughter of mine. She knows how to stick up for herself. I am really proud of her!" The Mexican-American male was not sure who had made a pass at his girl, but he was quite satisfied that justice had been done. The military policeman was at a loss.

1. Any new ideas about what really happened?
2. Why do you think this?

Have each group discuss briefly and give their ideas to the rest of the class and then read the following:

C: The daughter thought "Goodness, what a slap! I wonder who... and the policeman is an attractive man." The Mexican-American girl thought "Bah! All those whites are the same. Acting superior, but making passes at you anyway..." During the search, the purse was found in the pocket of the policeman's coat.

1. So, what actually happened?
2. Why do you think so?

Again, have each group report (briefly) to the entire class before reading the following:

D: Three people hugged themselves delightedly but without letting on:

- the white girl because of the kiss she had given to this delectable Mexican-American girl;
- the Mexican girl because of the slap she had given to this pawing thief of a policeman;
- and the Mexican man because of the trick he had played on the policeman.

Closure: Have the small groups return to the larger group and lead a discussion on the following questions: *Can you see to what extent the interpretations you have been giving are based on cultural stereotypes? The thoughts of the people in the train were based on stereotypes as well. Which stereotypes? How common are these stereotypes in daily life? What about yours? What did you learn or relearn about yourself?*

SECTION III
ACADEMIC SURVIVAL SKILLS

Academic Survival Skills (traditionally called Study Skills) have been a common topic of large group guidance units for many years. Their importance for school counselors and others stems from the fact that increased academic success in school directly correlates with an educator's overall goal of building self-esteem in students. Academic survival skill units also interrelate with other developmental guidance units such as decision making and communication units found elsewhere in this book. In addition, teachers who are hesitant to allow counselors to teach certain development guidance units tend to feel more comfortable when a counselor first teaches academic survival skills and then goes on to other less "academic" units. Many school counselors use such units as "enticements" to get their teacher colleagues interested in large group guidance units which deal with issues other than academic skills.

There is no doubt that knowledge and application of academic survival skills tends to increase a student's chances for school success. This is the reason that school counselors usually include an effective academic survival skills unit in their developmental guidance plan. Research indicates that an increase in school success corresponds directly to an increase in students' self-esteem. Higher self-esteem then leads to more success and the cycle continues. Above and beyond the increased self-esteem for students, increasing school success through the teaching of academic survival skills will also produce positive attitudes from school administrators, teachers, and parents toward the overall objectives of a developmental school counseling program.

An added benefit for students being involved in a counselor's academic survival skills unit is the inclusion of decision-making and communication skills within the unit. When teaching a study skills unit, topics such as being responsible for completing assignments, organizing your time or notebook, and test-taking skills are usually included. All of these topics involve some level of decision-making on the part of the student. In addition, when areas such as listening, following written or oral directions, and asking questions are addressed in an academic survival unit, students learn communication skills as well. Learning appropriate communication and decision-making skills tends to increase the chances for students' school success.

In addition to all the benefits for students, teaching a large group guidance unit focused on academic survival is beneficial for developing a positive understanding between counselors and teachers. There may be some teachers in your school who are hesitant to accept developmental group guidance as a legitimate part of a student's academic career. As noted above, such reluctant teachers are much more apt to view a unit on academic survival skills as more "justifiable" than certain other developmental guidance units found throughout this book. When these teachers accept a guidance unit as credible, they tend to view the counselor as more credible as well, and they are "hooked." This develops a more positive attitude toward the counselor and allows for the counselor to be more readily accepted into the classroom to conduct other guidance activities.

In summary, using the academic survival skills activities found on the following pages will help to increase students' self-esteem through improved school success, increase students' decision-making and communication skills, and promote a more positive relationship between counselors and those teachers who may be reluctant to have their students involved in developmental group guidance classes.

Activity 3.1

Time Management

Level:	Grades 6 to 9
Purpose:	For students to become aware of how they spend their time and to set up their own schedule to allow sufficient time for academics.
Materials:	"How Do I Use My Time" questionnaire and a "Planned Study Schedule" for each student.
Activity I:	You might begin by saying: *A lot of people say they don't have time for this or that, especially when it comes to homework. But, in most cases the time is there it's just not budgeted correctly. Now that you are in middle school you have a greater freedom in your use of time than when you were in elementary school. Today we are going to set up a schedule to help you manage your time. But before we do, let's see how you spend your time now.*
	Next, pass out "How Do I Use My Time" to each student. Ask them to work by themselves for 10 minutes and to make sure they include all their daily and weekly activities on the worksheet. When 10 minutes are up, ask the students to make a check by the category (jobs, homework, entertainment) to which they feel they need to devote more time. Then ask them to mark an "x" by the category to which they should devote less time. Then, ask the class to determine the appropriate amount of time that should be spent on academics (study) daily.
Activity II:	Pass out the "Planned Study Schedule." Then you might say: *Using a guide like the "Planned Study Schedule" is a good method for managing your time. First, fill in the activities you know you are going to be doing at certain times during the week (i.e., class time, piano lesson, basketball practice, TV, etc.). Then in the remaining squares, fill in an appropriate amount of homework study time, a time for chores, jobs which you need to get done, time for entertainment, and so forth. Remember, don't schedule homework time during your favorite TV program. Make sure you include more time for the category you feel you needed more time for and less time for the category you feel you needed less time to complete.*
Closure:	You might summarize by saying: *Today we have looked at how you use your time during the day. You have also decided what kind of activities you need more or less for. We have also established a set amount of time needed daily for homework and study. Even though it is good practice to set up a certain amount of time for study, remember that everyone is different and some may need more or less homework and study time than others.* Suggest to the students that they finish the Planned Study Schedule and adhere to it all next week as closely as they can.

How Do I Use My Time?

How do I spend my time? Do I have enough time to finish the things I want to do? What do I wish I had more time to do? Answer the following questions, estimating the time for things that you are not sure about:

I am responsible for the following chores at home:

      Chore   Time (minutes - daily, weekly)

_____

_____

I have a job outside my home: (Be sure to include irregular time slots, such as baby-sitting or yard work.)

      Job   Time (daily, weekly)

_____

_____

During the school year, I usually have homework to do. I spend the following amount of time doing it.

      Homework   Time (daily, weekly)

_____

_____

I belong to the following organizations or clubs that meet:

  Name of organization   Meeting time

_____

_____

I take lessons (music, sports)

      Activity   Time

_____

_____

I practice the following:

      Activity   Time

_____

_____

I spend the following time on entertainment (television, movies, shopping, time with friends, talking on the telephone, reading, riding my bike, etc.)

      Activity   Time

_____

_____

Planned Study Schedule

	Sun	Mon	Tues	Wed	Thurs	Fri	Sat
Morning							
9:00							
10:00							
11:00							
Noon							
1:00							
2:00							
3:00							
4:00							
5:00							
Evening							
6:00							
7:00							
8:00							
9:00							
10:00							
11:00							
12:00							

Class Schedule for _____(Fall) or _____(Spring) semester, 19_____.

Period	Class	Teacher	Room
1			
2			
3			
4			
5			
6			
7			

Activity 3.2

The Keys to Good Study

(May become two or more sessions)

Level:	Grades 6 to 12
Purpose:	For students to become familiar with the keys to good study habits which will, in turn, help them to become better students.
Materials:	"Study Rules" True/False list for individual student responses, "Homework Assignment Sheet" for each student, "SQ3R" handout for each student, "Commentary on Tips to Managing the Study Environment," and "Tips on Managing the Study Environment" handouts for each student. Also, you will need a pencil and paper for each small group to brainstorm and record responses. For Activity II, slips of paper with specific statements/questions may be given to each group.
Activity I:	Explain to students that most study skills that we learn are "self-taught" or not learned at all in a systematic way. This may be a big mistake because we can all profit from what other people know and have learned about how we learn. Although each person is a unique individual, there are certain true constants, e.g., having all the materials you know you will need at hand, be in the right mood to study, proper lighting, and so forth.
	Ask the students to volunteer other things (factors) they believe true for everyone. Do not get so far into this that it intrudes on the validity of the true/false questionnaire to follow. This sharing time should be to get everyone involved, to stimulate interest, and show the need for such an activity.
Activity II:	Hand out the questionnaire titled "Study Rules." Request the students to individually write T for True and F for False in the appropriate spaces. Let students know that after they've completed the questionnaire, the answers will be shared and discussed.

Answers: 1. T 2. F 3. T 4. F 5. F 6. T 7. T 8. T 9. F 10. T

Have the students find a partner and share their answers from the questionnaire. (It is best to have the partners decided before the activity begins.)

The purpose of having partners is to compare, to stimulate thinking, to encourage shared responses, and so forth. This helps to involve everyone.

Read each statement aloud and record on the board (you may have a student record) how many students answered True and how many answered False. Then read correct answers out loud. Discuss or summarize the results briefly.

Joe Wittmer, Ph.D. and Diane W. Thompson, M.Ed.

Activity III:	Small groups (prearranged) are given one of the six individual "Study Tips" below to discuss and brainstorm reactions and possible answers. Allow a maximum of ten minutes for distribution and brainstorming/discussion. Each group should have a recorder to write group responses during brainstorming. (The "Study Tips" should be written on individual slips of paper to give to each group.)
	Then ask the recorder of each group to share brainstormed group ideas and answers. Elicit comments from other class members as time permits.
Closure:	Summarize by reviewing the essentials on the study rules. Two or three rules may be selected for summary comments. The students may select those rules that they think most important and assist with the summary. Discuss the SQ3R study method with the entire group. Have a copy ready for each student. The students are encouraged to take home the SQ3R study method and apply it to some specific content area assignment within the week. This activity (method) is well enough defined on the handout that additional discussion should not be needed at this time. The students should return with results of the usefulness of this method and some discussion should follow at a later date (perhaps with the specific classroom teacher). Also, hand out to the students the Homework Assignment Sheet. Encourage the students to try using this form to keep track of their assignment for a week.

Study Tips

(positive attitude)

1. The importance of a positive attitude. What is it? How does it work?

(class expectations)

2. Do you know what is expected in your particular class? If not, how do you find out? Is it the same for everyone? Does the teacher give enough details? If not, how do you ask the teacher for more details?

(study partners
and/or study groups)

3. How important are "study partners" or "study groups?" What are they? How are they established? Maintained?

(organized notebook)

4. What does "organized" notebook mean? Is it the same for everyone? What are the essentials?

(physical and emotional)

5. How does your physical health and emotional well-being affect your work in school and study? Your anxiety regarding tests?

(established routine)

6. A routine is important. How does one establish one? Verify? Maintain? Keep record of, and so forth?

SQ3R—A Study Technique

S = SURVEY

Briefly look over the material you have to study. (Do a quick survey.). Read all the titles and subtitles. Look at the pictures, diagrams, maps, and so forth. If the selection is short, read the first sentence of each paragraph. If the selection is only one paragraph, read the first and last sentences.

Q= QUESTION

Write down some questions that your quick survey brought to mind. Think of questions that you expect the selection to answer.

Or, if questions have already been written, read through them carefully.

1st R = READ

Read the selection through carefully. As you read, notice the answers to the questions you wrote down (or the questions that were already written).

2nd R = RECITE

After you have finished reading, answer the questions. You may look back at the material whenever necessary.

3rd R = REVIEW

Briefly look back through the selection and remind yourself of the important points. This would be a good time to proofread your paper for accuracy while comparing your actions to the selection read.

This study technique is especially good for learning material in your textbooks. Whenever you have an assignment to read for any class, apply the SQ3R method. You will understand and remember more of the materials you read than if you simply "read" it.

Study Rules

In the list of "Study Rules" below, some are True and some are False.
Circle the "T" (for true) or "F" (for false) next to each rule.
(The correct answers were previously given.)

T   F   1. Try to study at the same time and in the same place every day.

T   F   2. Do the easy assignments first, then go on to the harder ones.

T   F   3. If you become tired while studying, take a break.

T   F   4. Always work on related subjects, one right after another.

T   F   5. Previewing upcoming chapters in your textbooks is a bad idea because you may become confused by too much information.

T   F   6. For each subject, keep two sets of notes, one for classwork and another for textbook information.

T   F   7. When reviewing for a test, quickly skim all your notes to get an overview. Then, go back and thoroughly review your notes to pick out specific details for memorization.

T   F   8. It is a good idea to keep all of your old tests and quizzes in every subject to use as review material for your final examinations.

T   F   9. Having a radio or TV playing in the background forces you to concentrate harder on what you are studying.

T   F   10. "Cramming" the night before an examination is a poor way to try to learn a subject.

Homework Assignment Sheet

Make a grid similar to this one and fill in your homework assignment for each class. You might ask your teacher to initial it to check to see if you got it correct.

Homework Assignment Sheet

Teacher Class	Assignment	Long-term assignment due date

Joe Wittmer, Ph.D. and Diane W. Thompson, M.Ed.

Commentary on Tips to Managing the Study Environment

1. Successful students study whether they feel like it or not. These students study because they know that study helps them reach their life goals. If you have difficulty in this area, perhaps you need some work with your counselor to find some career directions so you can see a relationship between your work in school and some goals ahead.

2. Students must learn to shift their minds into a study mode when study time comes around. Thoughts regarding worrying about the amount of homework ahead, dislike for teachers, or feeling sorry for one's self simply wastes valuable study time. Each time a person actually accomplishes successful study (when he or she sits down to do it) helps provide a positive mental habit for further study.

3. There are many things students can do for themselves to improve concentration—get rid of distractions, have study materials available, have definite time, and so forth. If there are problems understanding the materials, students should seek help from a teacher or tutor. When students have worries which prevent them from concentrating, they should seek help.

4. Study is not a social activity. Some students have difficulty being alone. Students should try to think of this time alone as an opportunity to know themselves better—who they are, what they're good at, how they feel regarding things they're learning, and so forth. Time studying alone can be productive times.

Tips on Managing the Study Environment

1. Find your best place(s) to study and go there each time.
2. Get rid of distractions—sounds, sights, interruptions.
3. Organize your study materials.
4. Work on building a positive attitude regarding the material.
5. Get down to business.
6. Train yourself to concentrate.
7. Learn to value time alone.
8. Reward yourself (a soft drink, or whatever) following a good study session.

Activity 3.3

Paying Attention

(Session one of three*)

Level: Grades 2 to 6

Purpose: To help students become aware of the impact of their non-verbal behaviors and to assist them in becoming more aware of attending skills that will help them achieve success at school.

Materials: Newsprint or chalkboard.

Activity I: Indicate to the students that they will be learning some ways that they can use to communicate more effectively by using their bodies. You may want to ask someone to send the rest of the group a message by only using a facial signal or other body language. Generate a list of ways to communicate nonverbally from students' ideas. These behaviors might include smiling, clenched fists, frowning, the OK sign, hands folded, and so forth. Make certain that you include sitting up straight (shows you are ready to listen or work), eye contact (lets the others know you are ready to listen), and leaning in. (Explain how this gesture conveys that you are ready to listen.) By using these skills they can become more successful in school. It is important for students to realize that teachers like to work best with students who pay attention.

Ask: *What does it mean when the teacher says, class, pay attention when I give directions?* Generate some ideas from the students and then put an asterisk (*) by "sitting up straight," "eye contact," and "leaning in" on the list already generated. Review each of these skills with a brief explanation as follows:

> *Sitting up straight means sitting nice and tall with a fairly straight back. It is not sitting so straight that you look like you would break, but also not so laid back that it appears you are not listening.*
>
> *Eye contact means looking at, but not staring at the person (teacher) who is talking.*
>
> *Leaning in implies leaning a little toward the talker (teacher) with your body.*

You may want to explain that each of these skills, in their own way, can help them become more successful students and that teachers know when a student is paying attention and ready to learn things.

Activity II: First, call a male from the class to be a model. Have him sit facing the class and you where all students can see him. Then, tell the students to watch the model as he uses eye contact with you and time him for 20 seconds while you talk to the class. Now call up a female model and have her demonstrate good eye contact for 20 seconds while you talk. Give positive reinforcement at the end of each model's demonstration. Explain that one can increase paying attention time with practice.

Ask the class what they noticed about the models as they were "paying attention." Teachers like to look out in the room and see which students are paying attention and giving good eye contact. Teachers want to know who is trying to learn. It makes them feel good about those students.

Joe Wittmer, Ph.D. and Diane W. Thompson, M.Ed.

Next, the female model demonstrates sitting up straight while using good eye contact. She is timed for 25 seconds and reinforced for her behaviors. The male model also demonstrates (for 25 seconds) sitting up straight and maintaining eye contact as the class watches. He receives positive reinforcement for these behaviors. Let them know that teachers notice who is sitting up straight and using good eye contact.

Instruct the male model to lean in a little as he sits up straight and uses good eye contact. The female model follows revealing the same three behaviors. Each is timed for 30 seconds and given positive praise. Ask the students what they noticed about the models, emphasizing the paying attention skills.

After the models have demonstrated all three skills and returned to their desks, discuss the demonstrations with the class.

Activity III:

Split the class into small groups (4 or 5 each) to practice the skills they've just viewed being modeled. Each group should play the "pay attention game" where each student will have a chance to sit up straight, lean toward the leader, and maintain eye contact as the models demonstrated.

The leader of each group should be the first timer. Explain to the students that they can use a watch or count to 15 by saying one, one thousand; two, one thousand, and so forth. All the other students in each group should look at the leaders (timers), sit up straight and lean toward them. After 15 seconds the leader reinforces the other students by saying: *You did a good job of paying attention for 15 seconds.* All group members should help each other learn to sit up straight, lean and use eye contact, or correct each other in a helpful manner regarding the skills. When the first leader finishes timing, explain that the next student to the left becomes the timer and instructs the group to pay attention for 20 seconds and then gives reinforcement for their having done this. This proceeds around the circle with each leader increasing the paying attention time by five seconds. The group should continue until you tell them that time is up.

Next, move the teams (groups) so that they are part of the larger discussion group. Discuss how things went in each small group. Discussion questions might include: *What was it like trying to use good eye contact with your leader? What were some of the things that helped you pay attention in the group? How do you think using these skills will help you in school? What are some things you can do to help yourself pay attention even if others around you are not?*

Closure:

Summarize by reinforcing the notion that paying attention at school can help students get better grades and that teachers will know by simply looking at them when they are concentrating and trying to learn. Indicate that they can start to use these skills today! Remind them to remember to sit up straight, lean forward, and give their best eye contact. Those who do this are on their way to being better students! Close by requesting that sometime today, or during the week, they practice paying attention to a friend or to their parents as they talk about something important to them.

*Adapted from Cuthbert, M. (1987). *Developmental guidance for school success skills: A comparison of modeling and coaching.* Unpublished doctoral dissertation, University of Florida, Gainesville.

Activity 3.4

Listening Carefully

(Session two of three)

Levels:	Grades 2 to 6
Purpose:	To help students become aware of how to listen for general ideas (content) and for feelings expressed; and, to assist students in learning the use of open-ended questions (what, now, when, or where) to clarify issues at school.
Materials:	None.
Activity I:	Remind them that last session they learned more about how to pay attention to the teacher and others. You may want to ask if anyone remembers the special things students can do to show that they are paying attention at school—sit up straight, use eye contact, and lean toward the talker. Reinforce students for the good listening skills they are using now as you talk and the ones that they used last time to remember the attention skills. Inform them they are going to learn more about listening and how it can help them become even better students.
Activity I:	Ask someone to tell the class about his or her favorite food. Choose someone and let that person talk for a few seconds. You might then respond to them with something totally off the subject, e.g., a student talks about pizza and you respond with: *I heard that the cost of shoes will going up in China.* The students will probably look confused and you might say that it takes more than your two ears to be an effective listener. Have the students discuss briefly what a good listener does—include things like pays attention to the speaker, thinks about what the person said, and says something to the person on the same topic.

Generate ideas from the students about how good listening is important in school. For example, a student would know the correct directions for assignments, when to line up for an activity or lunch, what ideas other kids were talking about, and so forth.

Explain that learning to listen to directions helps one to know what to do and how to become a successful student. And, if you listen for ideas and feelings of others you can learn new things. Sometimes in school you listen for facts or directions, when the teacher talks (e.g., "Do pages 101-103" or "Find the planet closest to the sun"), but, sometimes you listen for how others are feeling (e.g., "I'm scared about the math test" or I'm worried about my handwriting").

Explain that there are several things we can do to help us become better listeners and students. If we listen and do not understand, we can ask for more information by using questions that begin with what, how, when, or where. There are two kinds of questions that might help us think about things. One is an open question. The second is a closed question. Explain and demonstrate how a "yes" or "no" will answer most closed questions but that an open question encourages people to share more ideas, that an open question "invites" your teacher and others to share more.

Joe Wittmer, Ph.D. and Diane W. Thompson, M.Ed.

Do you like doing your math? (Closed)

How do you feel about doing your math? (Open)

Do we have to study for this test? (Closed)

What do we need to study for this test? (Open)

Does the test have essay questions on it? (Closed)

What type questions are on the test? (Open)

Indicate that knowing how to ask and answer questions like those above often clears up things that one does not understand.

Activity II:

Ask a male model to come to the front of the room and sit facing the class. Remind him to pay attention to you by sitting up straight, giving you eye contact, and leaning toward you as during the last session. Start a conversation about the playground at your school. Next, ask him to think about what is said and to ask an open-ended question about the topic (one that begins with what, how, when, or where). Continue the exchange for a few sentences to show that the model is listening. Demonstrate how one can listen for either content, feelings, or both. Reinforce the model. Ask the students how they know the model is listening and how teachers would know students were listening by the type of questions they ask.

Have a female model demonstrate the same listening and questioning techniques. That is, she will pay attention, listen to what has been said, and ask an open-ended question. Continue the conversation to show that each is listening to the other. Demonstrate listening for content and feelings. Again, reinforce the model and have the students point out the things they noticed that would indicate that the model was listening carefully to you.

After the models return to their seats, begin a large discussion group.

Activity III:

Divide the class into small groups and have each group member practice asking an open-ended question. In order to do this, explain that each student will need to pay attention to the speaker and think about what was said, so that they can ask a question about content and feelings. The starter should begin by talking about something that happened recently at school. The person on the starter's left will then ask an open-ended question (beginning with what, how, when, or where) about the ideas or the feelings that the first person had. Remind the group members to reinforce students asking the questions when they do them correctly by saying "good job" or "nice work." Group members should be encouraged to coach each other or help each other out if individual group members have trouble asking the questions. Each person in the circle asks the first starter an open-ended question. For the 15 minutes of practice time, the same pattern will continue with the next person to the starter's left talking about something related to school and group members asking open-ended questions of him or her around the circle again. Group members should continue to help or coach each other.

Move the teams so they are now part of the larger discussion group. Questions might include: *What was it like for you to use open-ended questions in your group? Tell some ways that you felt you were a good listener in your group. How do you think listening carefully at school will help you become better students? When might it be important to listen for feelings of others at school?*

Closure:

Summarize by indicating that good listening skills help us become better students. Remind them that listening means—paying attention to the speaker, thinking about what the person said, and saying something to the person on the same topic. Also, mention that often, an open-ended question is best because it reveals your interest in what the person is saying. Reinforce the notion that the use of these listening skills will help every one become more successful at school. Close by suggesting that during this next week they practice their listening skills and use some open-ended questions with their classmates, teachers, or parents to find out more about their ideas and feelings.

Activity 3.5

Volunteering Successfully

Level: Grades 2 to 6

Purpose: To help students learn how to volunteer ideas in class and to become more aware of coping mechanisms to overcome nervous feelings that inhibit their school performance.

Materials: Newsprint or chalkboard.

Activity I: Remind the students that in the previous two sessions they have learned how paying attention and being good listeners can help each of them become better students at school. Review the paying attention behaviors of sitting up straight, using eye contact, and leaning toward the speaker as well as the listening skills of paying attention to the speaker, thinking about what the person said, and saying something to the person on the same topic, e.g., asking open-ended questions that begin with what, how, when, or where. You might begin by explaining that today they are going to learn another way to help them become more successful as students. You might say: *Sometimes you have ideas but you do not share them with others. Sometimes you want to help teachers on special projects, but you do not let them know you are interested. Do you know what gets in the way of your doing what you want to do sometimes? It is often because of nervous feelings.* Indicate that today they will learn some ways to help overcome these nervous feelings and that those students who know how to share ideas and how to try new things tend to do better in school.

Next, ask someone to share a time that made them nervous at school. Facilitate any answers given. Help incorporate some of the following situations if the students do not generate them—giving a report in front of the class, taking a hard test, being called on when you are not sure of the answer, and so forth.

Ask: *What are some of the feelings you get in your body when you are nervous?* Generate a list on a chalkboard or newsprint. These might include: butterflies in your stomach, dry or cotton mouth, feel like you have to go to the bathroom, your heart beats faster, breathe faster, palms sweat, knees shake, hands quiver, talk too fast, and so forth.

Indicate that there are several ways to overcome these nervous feelings and teach them the following coping mechanisms:

1. Imagery—You might say: *Imagery or using your imagination can help you overcome nervous feelings that get in the way of your doing certain things. Thinking of safe places in your mind can help you relax. When you think of special safe places (like your own room at home, your tree house, grandma's house) your nervous feelings begin to fade away and you feel more in control of what you are needing to do. Just thinking you are calm can actually help you feel less nervous and help the butterflies go away.*

2. Deep Breathing—Explain that deep breathing or breathing in and out can help overcome nervous feelings too. Breathing in and out slowly three times helps one to relax. Indicate that as we breathe in and out our nervous feelings begin to go away and we feel more able to do what we need to do. *Just breathing in and out slowly can help us feel less nervous and more in control of ourselves. Sometimes it helps to see our lungs expand as we breathe in and how they get smaller as we breathe out.*

3. Self-Talk—You might say: *Self-talk or talking to yourself in positive ways can help you overcome certain nervous feelings. Telling yourself that you are going to be calm will help you feel more relaxed. Telling yourself that you can do something will help you actually do it. For example, telling yourself that you are going to do a good job on your report to the class today because you prepared it well will help you feel less nervous when you give it rather than telling yourself that you would be scared in front of the whole class. Talking to yourself in positive ways can help you feel less nervous and help you be more successful at school. Also, others have found it helpful to wear a rubber band on their wrists and to "snap themselves" each time they have a negative thought, or start to get nervous, and so forth.*

Activity II:

The first skill to be modeled should be the use of imagery. Ask a female model to come up front. Ask her to imagine and describe (out loud) a place that she goes to relax. Encourage her to tell all the sensations and feelings she has while she is describing her imagined place. Guide her to talk about the accompanying physiology—butterflies leave, breathe more slowly—whatever is true for her. Reinforce her. Relate to the class that this technique can work to calm them down so that they might be able to give a better speech, sign up for the class play, volunteer to read out loud in class, and so forth. (Since this is a difficult technique, the first model may not be able to give the best example and you may need to choose someone else who feels he or she could talk about an imagined place.) Proceed in the same manner with a male model.

The second skill to be modeled is the use of deep breathing. Have the male and female models in front of the class at the same time. Talk the models through breathing in slowly and releasing slowly for three times. Encourage the models to try to feel more relaxed each time they breathe in and out. Reinforce them by telling them to visualize their lungs filling up and emptying out and to be aware of the air entering their nose as they inhale. Ask the students what they noticed about the models as they demonstrated this technique. Let them know that students do better in school when they have a way of overcoming nervous feelings that sometimes get in the way of doing things the way they would like to do them.

The third skill to be modeled is self-talk. Have the models talk about what they could say to themselves to overcome their nervous feelings in a situation where they are told that they have to give a speech to two third grade classrooms—at one time. Guide them in the use of positive sentences on how they would prepare themselves for this task. Reinforce them. Choose who will demonstrate first by how ready each seems. Option: you demonstrate the use of the rubber band technique described above.

Conduct a discussion about their experiences with the modeling.

Activity III:

Break into small groups and appoint a leader for each group. The leaders should start by telling about a time when they felt very nervous about a school situation. Then they should tell what methods they use to overcome those nervous feelings. Next, the person on the left will tell about a nervous time and the way he or she chose to overcome nervous feelings. The second leader will guide the group in the practice of using imagery to overcome nervousness, the third leader will demonstrate deep breathing and the fourth leader should demonstrate self-talk to overcome nervousness as shown by the models.

Next, move the small groups back into the large discussion group and have them talk about their experiences. Some of your questions might include: *What was it like trying out ways to overcome nervous feelings?*

What did your group members do to make you feel comfortable trying out your new skills? How do you think these new skills might help you volunteer more ideas at school?

Closure:

Summarize by indicating that their ability to overcome nervous feelings at school is very important. Tell them that teachers respond in positive ways to students who volunteer to do things, are not afraid to ask good questions, and who appropriately share ideas in class. Remind them that when they feel those nervous feelings getting in their way, they now know what to do to overcome them—imagery, deep breathing, and/or self-talk. Close by suggesting they try to use one of the ways they've learned to overcome nervous feelings when they feel anxious or nervous. For practice, they might teach a family member one of the ways they learned to help themselves so that they can volunteer to do more things or share more of their ideas with others at school without becoming overly nervous.

Activity 3.6

Distractions in Listening and Learning: The Importance of Focusing on Listening

Level: Grades 4 to 9

Purpose: To help students understand that listening is an important skill needed to survive academically.

Materials: A copy of the True/False quiz for all participants, overhead projector, poster or chalkboard (covered up before class begins).

Introduction: Ask students to respond to these questions, in writing, and then follow with a discussion:

Can we do two things at once?

Is there a time when noise is a background filter instead of a background distraction?

Use the student responses to set the tone and introduce the activities in a manner similar to the following: *Today we are going to conduct a scientific experiment. We are all going to be involved in an activity that will either prove or disprove the following stated hypothesis—**Listening is a learned skill that requires concentration without distraction.***

When student curiosity and interest is set, begin Activity I.

Activity I: *As I read (story below), I want you to write directions to your home from the school's main entrance. Try to write quickly and give only important information. Raise your hand when you are finished. Now, begin.* (Begin reading aloud as if on television or radio, as the students begin writing. Remind them to keep writing.)

It is 7:00 a.m. It's a cold Tuesday morning and the temperature in (your town) is 42 degrees, the wind velocity is ten miles per hour, with gusts up to twenty miles per hour. There is no chance of (rain/sleet/snow) until Thursday evening or possibly Friday.

So, that's what's happening in our area. But, let's look at what is happening in Northern Ohio, specifically in the Cleveland area. The first snowstorm of the season! Snow began falling at 2:45 a.m. and three inches of the white stuff accumulated by 5:00 a.m. Then, three inches were added by 6 a.m. because of a fast-moving cold front from the lake. The temperature is 29 degrees, and it seems as if it will be snowing until nightfall.

Then, in your own words, say something like the following: *Now that you have been given the weather report, I will ask you to take the following short quiz. Please respond by filling in the correct time or numbers.*

NOTE: The quiz may be put on a poster or overhead before class or you or a student may read it at this time.

1. The newscast is at _____a.m. (7 a.m.)

2. The temperature in our town is _____degrees (42)

3. The wind velocity in our town is _____miles per hours. (10)

4. It may begin sleeting/raining/snowing in our town on _____. (Thurs. or Fri.)

5. In Cleveland, _____inches of snow have fallen according to the most recent record. (6)

6. The temperature in Cleveland is _____degrees. (29)

The students will give many good reasons for having done poorly on this quiz. But, basically, they found that they could not do two things at once. This is the point to be stressed. (Reduce their frustration by giving the correct answers to the quiz quickly.) See if anyone was able to get more than one or two answers and still succeed in writing directions to their home correctly and quickly. Allow discussion to limit frustration and focus on the main point of the experiment. Let the students quickly see that you were doing this on purpose to test the hypothesis. Ask the students: *Do you accept or reject the hypothesis?*

Activity II:

Read the exercise below. Three volunteers are needed who have agreed to hum or make other distracting noises while you read. With three students humming or singing softly, read the following:

George was totally exhausted after practice. What a drudgery—three tests, plus an extra game practice! Even thinking of his Saturday date with Joyce could not cheer him—he looked forward only to catching up on his sleep. Since George was so tired from late studying, he was grateful that Bob had planned to drive them home.

Ask the following questions related to the story. Conduct as you would any TRUE-FALSE quiz.

1. *George is on the football team. (T)*

2. *It is Friday. (T)*

3. *George has a date with Gloria on Saturday (F)*

4. *George and Bob are teammates. (T)*

5. *Bob has taken three tests. (T)*

6. *George was tired from studying. (T)*

Ask for student responses after giving correct answers. How many students answered 2 correctly? 3? 4?

Closure:

You might say: *Today, we have proven two things: 1) We can't listen effectively and do something else at the same time. 2) In order to listen effectively we can't have distracting noises or sounds. What can we do to improve our academic skills related to what we have learned today?* Write their responses on the board. Examples: Do not draw in class when you need to be listening to the teacher, study in a quiet place, turn the TV off when studying, take notes to focus your listening, and so forth. In your own words, summarize by saying something like: *In order to improve our academic skills, we all need to be better listeners, and it is a skill each of us can learn. We've listed some steps to take in order to listen and concentrate better in school. Think of one specific step you could take to improve your listening skills in class and try to implement it for one week. At the end of the week, check to see if your academic skills have improved.*

Activity 3.7

Learning Styles

Level:	Grades 5 to 9
Purpose:	For students to explore and survey their specific learning styles and study habits.
Materials:	Two student handout sheets (one for each student), "The Sixteen Keys" and "My Learning Styles (How I Study Best)." Pencils and paper for each group to use to brainstorm and record responses.
Activity I:	Give each student one minute to quickly write down the things they do when they "do homework at home." Specify "at home" since homework is often done at school. Explain to the students that they should write down things as they come to mind and not to worry about a specific order. (Examples: turn on music, find a quiet spot, sit at a table, lie on a bed.)

Then, ask the students to put their specific written list in rank order. The lists should not be rewritten. The items should be numbered in the rank order in which they would be done at home when preparing to study.

Example:

6   Open my textbook

7   Go over my class notes

10   Get a snack to eat

1   Sit down at a desk or table

5   Decide what to do first

2   Make sure I have everything I need

8   Do the first homework assignment

     (page, problem, paragraph, essay, etc.)

9   Check it over

3   Sharpen a pencil

4   Get notebook and/or paper

Ask one or two students (as time permits) to read their specific lists (just completed) to everyone. Write the items on the board as they are read and comment to reinforce the appropriate items as shared. Reinforcement should help students to focus on, 1) what is necessary, 2) what is wasted effort, 3) what leads to efficient homework study, and so forth. It can also be a way for you to make certain that everyone understands the task at hand and knows what to do to follow the instructions for the steps below. Invite student comments from other class members as the items are listed and reviewed.

Activity II:	Each student is then given a copy of the "Sixteen Keys." Make certain that each student understands the rating scale before they complete the "keys." (You may wish to file each student's "keys" in the respective "guidance" folders.)

Break the class into small groups of 4 or 5, appoint a leader, and ask them to discuss their respective responses to the "Sixteen Keys."

Closure:

After returning to the large group, you may ask: *What have we learned today? Have you learned something about yourself you did not know? How do your learning habits compare with your peer's habits?*

The Sixteen Keys

Rate yourself (honestly) on how often you try to do the following things:

Always	Most of the Time	Sometimes	Never	
❏	❏	❏	❏	1. Recognize what you don't know and agree to work on these areas.
❏	❏	❏	❏	2. Ask good, intelligent questions.
❏	❏	❏	❏	3. Work independently.
❏	❏	❏	❏	4. Have confidence in your academic ability.
❏	❏	❏	❏	5. Provide yourself with good study conditions.
❏	❏	❏	❏	6. Keep your supply of study equipment in good order.
❏	❏	❏	❏	7. Discover when and where you work best.
❏	❏	❏	❏	8. Work with time limits and use good time management.
❏	❏	❏	❏	9. Get your work done on time and handed in on time.
❏	❏	❏	❏	10. Use the libraries intelligently.
❏	❏	❏	❏	11. Know how to take effective notes.
❏	❏	❏	❏	12. Know how to plan and organize a term paper.
❏	❏	❏	❏	13. Deliberately increase your vocabulary daily.
❏	❏	❏	❏	14. Work on your memory skills.
❏	❏	❏	❏	15. Adequately prepare for tests.
❏	❏	❏	❏	16. Know your study time limits.

Activity 3.8

Managing Your Study Time

(May be adapted to two consecutive sessions)

Level:	Grades 7 to 12
Purpose:	To develop knowledge of, and skills in, managing time—both long-range and short-range.
Materials:	The "Learning Survey" Pre-test, "Tips for Managing Study Time," and the "Daily Activity List." Have copies available for each student.
Activity I:	Ask the students for a show of hands on how many of them could make better use of their time? How many need instruction on time management? Explain that study skills are not inborn but are taught and that most people need "refresher" courses from time to time. Then, hand out the pretest (Learning Survey). Allow time to complete it. Then, tally their responses on the board (using a show of hands) and discuss the correct answers briefly. (All answers are "false.")
Activity II:	Next, you might say: *The skill we will be working on today is time management. This is a life skill which will always be needed. We must start with the fact that we each have only 24 hours in a day. Some of that time is structured for us, like sleep, school, and so forth. However, each of us has several hours each day about which we make our own personal decisions. Some students begin with the assumption that 7 1/2 hours of school per day is enough and that they shouldn't have to study outside of school. They choose to work or spend time with their friends to the exclusion of any study time. Those students who choose to continue to do little or no homework will have minimal success with this activity—or with school! This experience is designed for students willing to spend some time and wanting to make the best use of that time.*
	Next, hand out "Tips for Managing Study Time" and break the class into small groups. Appoint a recorder for each group to lead the discussion on these points. After about 15 minutes, lead a large group discussion on these points. An alternative may be to assign each small group a specific "tip" to report on (back to the larger group).
Closure:	All of us, but especially students, will benefit from instituting and using a time management plan for studying. However, it is very important that all students "plan" to study. As someone once said: "No one plans to fail, but many fail to plan." Close by passing out the daily "Activity List" and ask students to complete it for today. You may wish to explain the different columns.

Joe Wittmer, Ph.D. and Diane W. Thompson, M.Ed.

Learning Survey
TRUE OR FALSE QUIZ

T   F   1. It's best to study for all classes in the same way.

T   F   2. You should study hard the day before a big test so you won't forget anything.

T   F   3. If you're having a hard time with your subjects, you just need to spend more time studying the material.

T   F   4. It doesn't matter where you study as long as you have variety.

T   F   5. Once you have a good study plan, you'll never have to change it.

T   F   6. You will learn much more by copying your notes over.

T   F   7. A student of average abilities cannot get better than average grades.

Commentary on "Learning Survey"

All answers are false.

1. There are classes in which you must understand the big picture, like a history class; other classes require exact procedures and much detail, like math class. Therefore, you study differently for different subjects.

2. The best way to remember things is to review it first within 24 hours after exposure and then regular review until testing occurs. Major study delayed until test time results in little real learning but much forgetting.

3. The quality of study time is much more important than quantity.

4. A regular place to study increases the likelihood that you will be in a "study mood" when there. Also, you have excellent lighting and study materials all in one place and you won't have to be searching for pens, paper, and so forth.

5. You may have a class in which your study plan doesn't work and you'll want to change. There are many variations in methods of studying.

6. There are many things you should do to notes—place key facts on flash cards for study, for example. However, simply recopying them results in very little learning. Saying them into a tape recorder for later listening is often very helpful.

7. Better grades come as a result of many factors. Most people have average abilities—some of those with average abilities make superior grades; others make very poor grades. Appropriate study skills can make a big difference.

Tips for Managing Study Time

1. Keep a daily activity list—to-do notes.
2. Set a regular time to study.
3. Study in manageable increments of time—find your attention "limits."
4. Study the more difficult subjects first.
5. Review each subject often.
6. Learn to "steal" time for study (i.e., use a tape recorder and listen while eating).

Daily Activity List

DATE _____

MUST DO!	SHOULD DO!	COULD DO!
1. _____	1. _____	1. _____
2. _____	2. _____	2. _____
3. _____	3. _____	3. _____
4. _____	4. _____	4. _____
5. _____	5. _____	5. _____
6. _____	6. _____	6. _____
7. _____	7. _____	7. _____
8. _____	8. _____	8. _____
9. _____	9. _____	9. _____
10. _____	10. _____	10. _____

Joe Wittmer, Ph.D. and Diane W. Thompson, M.Ed.

Commentary on "Tips to Managing Study Time"

1. A priority activity list is the clearest way to see where the time goes. Face the truth about yourself and how you spend your time. Your time management plan should be built around the activity schedule.

2. We humans are creatures of habit. It is easier to study once regular study times have become a habit. Once this habit is established, students find that they waste less time and mental energy on deciding when to study, on avoiding studying, and on complaining about the studying that needs to be done.

3. A manageable increment may require different lengths of time for different individuals. The maximum should be about an hour before taking a short 5- to 10-minute break and rewarding yourself with something (e.g., a snack or whatever). Students whose study habits are poorly established should begin with about 20-minute increments. Regardless of the length of the time increment, it should be used for study only. Students should concentrate on study for just that segment of time, regardless of the additional work that will be needed later. This time should be free of any distractions. Then, take a short break and return for the next increment as soon as possible. Studying between several lengthy telephone chats does not constitute a night of study and is poor time management.

4. Unless you have a pressing project with a due date just around the corner, study your least favorite subject first. When you begin to feel tired, it will not be as difficult to complete the easier assignments with the more difficult one behind you.

5. Research reveals that people learn best when they review often. Studying a subject 15 minutes each of five nights will have more benefit than studying 1 1/2 hours once per week. Not keeping up your subjects on a daily basis is one of the most costly mistakes students make.

6. Find short amounts of time which you can "snatch" some study time. If dinner is late, use the waiting time for study. Give up a TV show which you don't really enjoy anyway. While waiting for the orthodontist, while riding to appointments (providing you're not driving!), weekends, or even getting up thirty minutes early some mornings—all are possibilities for "stealing" extra time. And, if you tape record your notes (or summaries of your readings) listen to them during snack times, in your car stereo, and so forth.

Activity 3.9

Following Directions

Level:	Grades 2 to 6
Purpose:	To teach students the importance of following directions to enhance school success.
Materials:	"Following Directions" handout for each student.
Activity:	Pass out copies of the "Following Directions" handout (face down). Tell the students that they will have five minutes to complete the test. Then, have them turn their individual papers over and begin. After five minutes, say: *Stop!* and discuss the questions given below:

    a. How did you feel when you discovered the "trick?"

    b. What did you learn from the activity?

    c. How do you feel about tests?

    d. What happens to you before and during a test?

    e. How do you get ready for tests?

    f. What are some reasons for having tests?

    g. How did the noise/outbursts affect your concentration?

Closure:	Close by indicating that following directions is very important when taking tests. Then read each item on the "test" and ask for a show of hands on those who responded to the item correctly. Lead a discussion on each item.

Following Directions

Name _____

1. Read everything before doing anything.

2. Put your name in the upper right-hand corner of the page.

3. Circle the word "name" in sentence 12.

4. Draw five small squares in the upper left hand corner of this paper.

5. Put an "X" in each square.

6. Put a circle around each square.

7. Put a circle around sentence 7.

8. Put an "X" in the upper right hand corner of this paper.

9. Put a triangle around the "X" you just made.

10. On the back of this paper, multiply 733 x 60.

11. Draw a rectangle around the word "circle" in sentence 7.

12. Loudly call out your first name when you get to this point.

13. If you think you have followed directions carefully to this point in the test, call out "I have."

14. On the reverse side of this paper add 89 + 9305.

15. Put a circle around your answer, then put a square around the circle.

16. Count out in a normal speaking voice from one to ten backwards.

17. Punch 3 small holes in the top of this paper with your pencil point.

18. If you are the first person to get this far, call out "I am first."

19. Underline all even numbers up to ten on this

20. Say out loud "I am nearly finished."

21. Now that you have finished reading carefully, do only sentences one and two.

Activity 3.10

The Pros and Cons of Studying

Level: Grades 3 to 6

Purpose: To allow students to make value decisions pertaining to study.

Materials: Copy of Script for two players, 5 x 7 cards for each group with a problem situation written out for each group.

Activity I: You might say: *The real question is not always **not to** study, sometimes it includes **when, where,** and, occasionally, even **if**.... Do we always need to study... for everything? Do the same rules always apply?*

Next, call for a short dramatization between two players. The students should receive the Script a few minutes before the activity begins. Ask Jerome and Jake to perform the skit below entitled, "To Study or Not to Study."

Script: To Study or Not to Study

Jake was talking to his friend Jerome on the phone when Jerome reminded him of their big test in social studies tomorrow.

Jake: *Oh, no, My dad promised to take us to see "Jarassic Park" tonight. I've wanted to see that movie since last spring, and I know I'll never talk him into going again.*

Jerome: *Well, it's your grade, Jake. But, remember, Mr. Moore said that this would count one-third of our 9-weeks grade, and you've got a "C" going right now. You had better think about this one. Doesn't your dad ground you for two weeks for every grade you get below a "B"?*

Ask the students to write a short comment on the dramatization. Then place them in groups of 4 or 5. In small group follow-up, ask the students to share what they felt Jake's solution should be and to brainstorm what they think the results of not studying should be—should it be self-punishment, parent "grounding"—should it always mean something negative? Then, have them answer each question as if they were parents and/or teachers. What action would they take when poor results in a class obviously were the result of "not studying"?

Joe Wittmer, Ph.D. and Diane W. Thompson, M.Ed.

Activity II: Give each of four groups one of the problem situations listed below. Allow ten minutes (maximum) and ask each group to define their problem and to develop a short, creative skit that will best reveal their solution.

Problem Situations

1. You have an important test tomorrow in your math class for which you have not yet studied. When you get home from school you find out that your mother wants to take you to see a good movie. She does not know that you have a test tomorrow. What would you do?

2. Your grades have been dropping and you decide that you want to start studying at home every day. How will you tell the other members of your family that you need time and a place to be alone for studying?

3. You didn't understand the directions, but it seems like the rest of the class did. Show how you would ask a teacher for extra help in one of your classes.

4. You received a "D" on your report card in one of your classes. You thought you were going to get a better grade. Show how you would ask your teacher about it.

Have each group read their problem and then perform their "solution skit." Request that they have a member of the group play each role as required in the situation, i.e., teacher, student, and so forth.

Closure: You might say: *We have learned today that we all have to make decisions on when and if we are going to study. We have to make that decision for ourselves. No one can force us to read or study. But, remember if we choose not to study we have to face the consequences of not being prepared, not having our homework completed, and so forth.*

Activity 3.11

Study Time

Level: Grades 7 to 12

Purpose: To help students become more aware of effective study habits.

Materials: Copies of "How I Study Best" for each student.

Activity: Begin by saying: *Let's make a list* (ask someone to write on the board as list is generated by class members) *as if we were going to write a "Dear Ann Landers" advice column on "How to get the most out of study time."*

It is best to remain open to student comments and accept any novel ideas if and when they are presented. Emphasis should be on everyone examining their own study/homework/learning habits to *improve* their respective study habits. Indicate that everyone—yes, even school counselors—needs to improve on something. Improvement may be accomplished—like most things in life—one step at a time. There is an old saying: "Always eat an elephant one bite at a time." This can be applied to any assignment given you at school.

Now, ask each student to read and respond to the twelve questions on the handout, "How I Study Best." Then place them in small groups, giving them an opportunity to share their responses. Have the small groups return to the larger group and lead a discussion on their overall feelings regarding what they've learned from this activity.

Closure: Emphasize that this activity is important and that a follow-up session with each of them can be scheduled to go on to the next logical steps:

1. Helping them to take steps to improve to get the most out of study time.

2. And, to monitor what results they've had.

Joe Wittmer, Ph.D. and Diane W. Thompson, M.Ed.

How I Study Best

1. Does background noise **help** or **interfere** with your ability to study? (circle one)

2. Do you study best with **low** or **high** lighting? (circle one)

3. Do you prefer studying **sitting upright** in a chair or **lying down** on the couch or bed? (circle one) (or somewhere else _____)

4. Do you have a strong interest to learn the material you will have to study? (Yes____ No_____)

5. How long can you work at an assignment before giving up? (hours_____ minutes_____)

6. Do you take responsibility for **your own** studying or do you need **someone to help** you study? (circle one)

7. Do you have a regular schedule or time that you study each day? (yes____ No____ sometimes_____)? (weekends: yes____ No_____ sometimes_____)?

8. Do you study best **with peers, alone, in a pair, in a team** or **with adult supervision**? (circle one)

9. How do you learn best—**by seeing things, listening to things, by doing,** or **by reading**? (circle one)

10. Do you need to **eat** or **drink, nibble** or **be slightly hungry** while studying? (circle those that apply)

11. What time of day do you prefer to study_____?

12. How much room do you need to move around in during study time (**very little, average, a lot**)? (circle one)

Activity 3.12

Coping with Stress at School: Using Relaxation and Imagery

Level: Grades 4 to 12

Purpose: To help students learn better study techniques, relaxation techniques when anxious, and to be better prepared and less anxious about taking tests, and so forth.

Materials: Have copies of "Muscle Relaxation" and the "Simple Form of Relaxing" handouts available for each student; newsprint, and felt tip pens.

Activity I: You might say: *A lot of people get nervous and feel anxious when they are about to take a test. What is anxiety?* (Let someone define this for the class.) *We tend to get anxious about tests from four concerns:* (Have these written on the board prior to beginning this activity.)

1. *Concerns about how others will view us if we do poorly.*

2. *Concerns arising from threats to our own self-image.*

3. *Concerns about future security.*

4. *Concerns about not being prepared.*

These concerns can trigger bodily reactions such as not being able to sleep or eat before a test. Also, test anxiety can disrupt your thoughts while taking a test so you can't concentrate well or you blank out what you've studied. Today we are going to do two activities that will help us relieve our test anxiety so we can do our best on the tests we need to take.

Next, divide the class into small groups. Tell each group to come up with four or five ways in which students can be better prepared for tests so that they will feel less anxious going into the test. Give them an example from the list and then move around the room from group to group helping them come up with ideas—ask them to brainstorm, to be creative! Have them write their answers on large newsprint (using felt tip pens) and tape them up on the wall. After five minutes, have each group explain their papers. The list of ways to be better prepared will most likely include some of the ideas below:

1. Make sure you know what kind of test you're taking (multiple choice, essay, etc.).

2. Take good, clear notes during class.

3. Make an outline of the chapters the test will cover.

4. Explain the information you need to know into a tape recorder using your own words. Play it back while you are getting ready for school, and so forth.

5. Begin studying earlier, not just the night before—stop procrastinating!

6. Take study breaks to exercise.

7. Mnemonic devices. (You may have to explain this one.)

8. Learn to relax.

Joe Wittmer, Ph.D. and Diane W. Thompson, M.Ed.

Activity II:

You might say: *One of the most important ways to relieve test anxiety is by learning to relax. Relaxation can be achieved by using your imagination. We are going to try to use our imagination today to learn to relax.*

Ask the students to become comfortable in their chairs and to close their eyes. Tell them to listen carefully while you read (and to picture in their mind) what you are saying. However, ask them not to focus on your words, i.e., just hear what you say and not to concentrate on your words. Read the following, pausing several seconds between sentences giving students time to bring the images to mind.

Close your eyes, settle back in your chairs and imagine that you are in the cockpit of a spaceship preparing for take off. Take a slow, deep breath, inhaling through your nose as you imagine yourself breathing pure oxygen in the cockpit. Hold your breath for a moment and imagine the power you feel as the spaceship takes off. Exhale slowly as you relax knowing that your space flight has begun and visualize your lungs emptying out. Feel your chest and body relax as you sink deeper into your chair. Take another deep breath of the pure oxygen, inhaling through your nose and visualize your lungs filling up. Then exhale slowly. Now, let yourself breath normally and let the "air breathe you." Become aware of your body. Feel your feet and legs. Imagine them becoming very heavy as the force of gravity pushes you down. Imagine your back and shoulders, arms, hands and head becoming very heavy. The force of gravity has made them too heavy to lift. As your spaceship proceeds into space, imagine what it would be like to move into outer space. Imagine yourself drifting weightlessly. Imagine the deep, pure blue color of space all around you. Imagine how the earth looks far off in the distance, getting smaller and smaller as you relax more and more. Imagine stars and planets moving past you in the distance. Now, imagine yourself moving into a space of bright white light. You are approaching a star. As you draw closer, you are surrounded by its glow. Imagine feeling warm and comfortable as you relax in the glow of the star. If disturbing thoughts or feelings enter your mind as you enjoy the feeling of being surrounded by the warm bright light of the star, allow them to pass by you just as you imagine planets and stars passing you by on this voyage. Let these thoughts and feelings fade into the distance, leaving them behind you in the same way that you imagine a comet disappearing over the horizon. Now, slowly open your eyes.

Closure:

Have a few students share their experience with the class and use your best facilitative counseling skills —do not give untimely advice, do not interpret, and so forth. Then, tell the students: *You can use this technique yourself. You may want to create another image which may relax you, such as: imagine yourself horseback riding along the beach, water-skiing on a calm, beautiful lake, skiing down a frosted white mountain, floating in a boat in a calm lake, floating over the beach in a large blue bubble, and so forth. When should you use your imagination to relax?* (the night before the test, that morning before you go to school, a short imagery trip right before the test) *Sometimes it helps to imagine taking the test and doing well on it. That is, see yourself calm, confident and doing well!* Then, give each student a copy of the fantasy you just had them experience. You might say: *Today we have discussed ways to be more relaxed and prepared for tests. We have come up with specific ways to study* (refer to the lists on the wall) *and we have learned a way to relax through imagery.* Then, give the students the "Muscle Relaxation" and the "Simple Form of Relaxation" handouts. Suggest that before they take a test in the upcoming week that they try doing the "Muscular Relaxation" and the meditation exercise from the handouts.

Muscle Relaxation

Begin by finding a spot on a bed or chair and getting really comfortable. Tell yourself, "I am going to relax completely and let all my tension just float away."

1. Take a deep breath and hold it (count backwards from 5 to 0). Exhale slowly letting yourself become like a warm, wet rag-doll all over as you relax. Repeat to yourself.

2. Tense your right arm and hand and make a fist. For 20 seconds, keep the arm tense and every other body muscle relaxed. Breathe regularly and slowly. Then slowly, relax that right arm. Notice that it feels loose, limp, and heavy. Repeat the "tensing" for 20 seconds.

3. Do the same with the left arm. Notice how the tension flows out when you release it. Repeat the tensing for twenty seconds and relax. Spend a minute letting your whole body relax.

4. Focus attention next on your right leg. Tighten as many muscles as you can. Hold the tension making sure that all other muscles are relaxed and that you are continuing to breathe regularly. After 20 seconds, release the tension. Notice the relief as the tension flows away.

5. Repeat for the left leg.

6. Now tense your left arm and right leg. Keep all other muscles relaxed. Hold them for 20 seconds. Then relax. Let your whole body drift into deep, deep relaxation.

7. Now tense your right arm and left leg. Hold the tension. Be sure that you're breathing regularly and that all other muscles are relaxed. Release all tension and let relaxation flow in to take its place.

8. Now contract the muscles in your lower back and arch your back. Hold this tension for 20 seconds. Release the tension. Notice how relaxed your body feels.

9. Now shrug your shoulders as if you are trying to touch your ears. Hold this until you feel an aching in your shoulder muscles. Allow your shoulders to move down, way down, and feel the relaxation. Check to see if all your muscles are heavy and relaxed.

10. Now push your head back on your chair or pillow. Contract those muscles in the back of your head and neck by pushing against the chair or pillow. Keep all other muscles relaxed in your arms, legs, and back. Now release the tension letting your neck muscles completely relax as deeply as you can.

Joe Wittmer, Ph.D. and Diane W. Thompson, M.Ed.

A Simple Form of Relaxation

Find a comfortable place where you won't be disturbed for 10 to 20 minutes and follow these directions. Once a day works best.

1. Sit comfortably and quietly.

2. Tell yourself that you are going to use the next 10 to 20 minutes to relax yourself.

3. Surrender the weight of your body, allowing the chair, or floor to support you.

4. Close your eyes, gently cutting out all visual distraction.

5. As you inhale, repeat to yourself: "I AM..."

6. As you exhale, repeat "RELAXED." Practice this. Repeat several times.

7. Continue to breathe normally—not trying to change it in any way. Just visualize it happening and continue to repeat: "I AM" with inhalation; "RELAXED" with exhalation.

8. As your mind wanders, gently bring it back to the awareness of your breath as it enters your nose and back to your statement; "I AM RELAXED."

9. Continue doing this for as long a time as you have established (15 to 20 minutes minimum).

10. To conclude, discontinue the phrase and slowly stretch your hands and feet, your arms and legs, your whole body.

11. Open your eyes a sliver at a time—like the sun coming up in the morning and continue on your way.

Activity 3.13

Taking a Test: The Many Factors Involved

Level:	Grades 3 to 7
Purpose:	To allow students to explore more good test taking skills.
Materials:	"Your Testing Pulse" handout, a worksheet listing the different kinds of tests and pencil and paper for small group brainstorming.
Activity I:	Introduce this activity as follows: *The word "test" almost always causes an emotional reaction. Let's look at a continuum....* (Write the continuum on the chalkboard.) Explain the continuum.

HARRIED HARRY...COOL CAL

*What is the first word that comes to mind when I say the word **test**????*

Write the word down.

Now look at that word. Think about it. Put yourself on the continuum. Where do you belong?

Most people don't really understand that taking a test is a learned skill. There are certain procedures or steps to follow, certain things to do, that will help all of us have a less negative response to tests.

Learning these techniques does not guarantee that you'll make a 100% on every test you take in the future... but it does assure you that you'll raise your test-taking potential to its highest.

Next, distribute the handout, "Your Testing Pulse." Allow time for the students to respond with pencil (individually) to this questionnaire. (Allow 5 minutes maximum.)

After the students are finished, divide them into small groups and ask them to share one or two of their answers to the questionnaire. Then ask them to answer in a go-around: *1) The best experience you've ever had with a school test, and 2) The worst experience you've ever had with a test.*

You might say: *In most cases students want to do well on tests. You have good feelings when you do well on a test. How can we better prepare ourselves so we can make high scores on a test and feel good about ourselves academically? I'm going to assign each group a type of test (multiple choice, true/false, matching, essay, fill-in-blank, short paragraph response). Each group should come up with 3 to 5 "Helpful Hints" on how to study for, and to take this kind of test. Write them down on the newsprint.* (Example: On a multiple choice test, first eliminate the answers you know are wrong.). *You'll have about 7 minutes. Begin.* (Note: You will want to walk from group to group helping them to come up with ideas. Have them write their hints 2 inches in height—use felt tip pens.)

When time is up, have one student from each group explain their "Helpful Hints" to the class. It will work best if they tape their respective newsprint's to the wall.

| **Closure:** | You might say: *Today we have had only a short time to unravel the mystery of test-taking, but we have made an important first step by coming up with hints to help us study for and to take tests feeling better prepared. This week find out more about the type of test your group was assigned by asking teachers, parents, and friends about how they would take such a test. Write them down and we'll add them to our list next time we discuss test taking.* |

Your Testing Pulse

Yes   No   1. Do you feel good when you do well on a test?

Yes   No   2. Do your parents feel good when you do well on a test?

Yes   No   3. Do your teachers feel good when you do well on a test?

Yes   No   4. Do your peers feel good when you do well on a test?

5. Of the four people listed above, whose opinion is most important to you? _____

_____

6. Of the four, whose opinion is least important to you? _____

_____

7. If you have two or more "No's," what would you like to change? ____

_____

8. How do you feel when a test is announced and you have to prepare for it? _____

_____

9. How do you feel when you begin to take a test? _____

_____

10. Before taking a test, what questions would you like to ask the teacher? _____

_____

Activity 3.14

Tips for Successful Test Taking

Level:	Grades 5 to 12
Purpose:	To learn some creative "tips" on how to take tests.
Materials:	Handouts of the "Tips for Test Taking" for each student.
Activity:	The following test-taking tips can be used in a variety of ways to familiarize students with effective test taking skills. Be creative in ways in which you help students learn these test taking tips. Some counselors have used the small group approach (with an appointed recorder for each group summarizing the most important points) while others have used a large group discussion approach. Some have been successful in having students develop "rap" songs using the words while others have used student designed skits to get the "tips across to students." However, dividing up the handout assigning parts to different small groups to later report to the larger group tends to work best.
Closure:	Regardless of your method (be creative and as non-boring as possible), always summarize the main points and give everyone a chance to participate if they so desire.

Joe Wittmer, Ph.D. and Diane W. Thompson, M.Ed.

Tips for Testing

1. Avoid any distractions. If possible, don't sit where you might be distracted. If, during the test you find something bothering you, ask the teacher if you might move.

2. Always read directions thoroughly—even though you've done that particular kind of test before and think that you know what they say.

3. If you are nervous, take a couple of deep breaths—it helps.

4. You may want to first answer the questions to which you know the answers and do the harder ones later.

5. Remember that your first hunch is usually correct. Your mind files away information and although you cannot consciously recall it, your subconscious may be working for you.

6. Don't look for answers to fall in a pattern—they usually don't.

7. Don't spend too much time on any one question. Use your time wisely, especially on a timed test.

8. Watch for related questions which may help you get other answers.

9. Watch the English usage. Sometimes a clue to the correct answer may be whether it makes sense grammatically.

10. Pay attention to the scoring system to see if you are penalized for wrong answers. If the examiner says "do not guess" it means that you will be penalized for wrong answers. In this case, if you have no idea of the correct answer, leave it blank; if you can make an educated guess, do so. If there is no penalty for wrong answers, attempt to answer every question; if you have no idea of the correct answer, mark the answer that seems most reasonable to you.

11. Remember to bring the "tools" you will need (paper, pencils, etc.).

12. Choose a good seat for a clear view of the board if need be.

13. Make yourself comfortable in your chair.

14. Always read directions carefully.

15. Think before writing.

16. Take a few rest pauses during the test.

17. Be prepared! Study. Know what the test will be covering.

18. Be well-rested and thinking positively!

Multiple-Choice Tests

1. Read the main part of the question, think of a possible answer, then look for it. Read all the choices.

2. Use the process of elimination. If you cannot think of the right answer, read all the choices, delete those that are obviously incorrect, and then choose from those remaining.

3. Look for qualifying statements and/or words in the stem (main part) or in the answer. You can usually delete answers with qualifying words such as always, all, none, never, not.

4. Be aware that there may be more than one correct answer. Don't stop reading when you have found a correct answer. Choices D or E may read "B and D" or "All of the above." If you notice such choices, reread the entire statement and all the choices to be sure.

Essay Tests

What does essay mean? It is a well organized written discussion of a specific topic. Your teacher will grade you on how well you know the facts and how well you are able to write about the facts you know.

Planning is the key to a successful essay test. The following should be taken into account when planning your answer.

1. Reread the directions so that you will know exactly what is asked.

2. Answer just what is requested.

3. Outline your answer on scratch paper first.

4. Organize your outline:
    a. Don't include too much.
    b. Keep your notes short.
    c. Watch your time.

5. Adding the filling:
    a. Show main points as headings.
    b. Give examples and illustrations.
    c. Avoid "padding."
    d. Include special information.

6. Check and double-check your paper for the following errors:
    a. Omitted words (may change word meaning).
    b. Wrong references (to people and places).
    c. Arithmetic errors (in math or science).
    d. Incorrect formulas (in math or science).
    e. Improper punctuation (may change meanings).
    f. Errors in grammar.
    g. Careless spelling (like there for their).
    h. Reversals (as "1942" for "1492").

True-False Tests

1. Be suspicious of very broad statements containing the key words ALWAYS or NEVER. These words can often make the statement false, even though it may sound true.

2. Be on the lookout for one small word or phrase that may spoil an otherwise true statement.

Completion Questions

1. Watch the number of blank spaces. Two blank spaces call for two words, three blank spaces for three words.

2. See if the sentence gives any clue; for example, does the verb call for a singular or plural form?

3. If you can't think of the exact word, do not leave the space blank. Try a less correct answer, for it may earn part credit.

Standardized Tests

1. Use a No. 2 pencil only.

2. Carefully fill in the appropriate bubble on the answer sheet—be neat and make your marks dark. They are machine graded.

3. Be sure you're marking on the correct portion of the answer sheet and your answer number matches up with the test item number.

4. Don't make stray marks on the answer sheets which may cause your answer sheet to be "thrown out" by the machine.

5. Raise your hand if you don't understand the directions.

6. Do your best! Decisions sometimes are based on your score.

Activity 3.15

Preparing for a Test

(Adapted from an activity created by Patty Vincent)

Level:	Grades 1 to 5
Purpose:	To reduce a student's stress and increase scores on tests by familiarizing them with eight things they can do to be ready for a standardized testing situation.
Materials:	"Getting Ready for a Test" handout copies for each student.
Activity 1:	Begin by asking the students what feelings they experience when you say "test." Briefly discuss test anxiety and how it can reduce test scores. Tell your students that today you will focus on how they can reduce their test anxiety.

Next, hand out "Getting Ready for A Test" and discuss each of the eight areas, having the students tell you what they think the reasons are for each area's importance.

1. GET A GOOD NIGHT'S SLEEP—Students draw themselves in bed.
2. EAT A WARM, NUTRITIOUS BREAKFAST—Students draw a nutritious breakfast on a plate.
3. DO YOUR VERY BEST—Students draw a picture of themselves doing what they do best (Example: math, riding horses, etc.).
4. BRING 2 SHARPENED #2 PENCILS—Students draw 2 pencils.
5. BE PRESENT AND ON TIME THE DAY OF THE TEST—Students put the hands on the clock.
6. BE A GOOD LISTENER DURING THE TEST—Students draw big ears on the face.
7. COLOR THE CIRCLE DARK AND ROUND—Students fill in one circle dark with pencil.
8. BE REAL QUIET AND DON'T DISTURB OTHERS—Students draw a picture of themselves being real quiet (tip toeing, saying "sh-h-h," etc.).

Have the students form a triad and have them share some of their respective drawings as much as they feel comfortable doing.

Joe Wittmer, Ph.D. and Diane W. Thompson, M.Ed.

Next, discuss how relaxing before a test can help a student's score as well. Then have the students close their eyes and imagine the following:

Imagine you are floating in a dark room... you can't feel or see anything around you... then you notice a light in the distance... float towards the light... you see now that it's a door to the outdoors... the door opens into a grassy field... go through the door out into the field... it's a beautiful, warm day... now allow your body to float down into the grass... the sun feels so good... you notice there are several animals off in the distance— one of them is a baby elephant walking towards you—you realize the elephant is going to accidentally step on you so you tighten up your stomach... but he turns around the other way, you relax... he turns back around—tighten up your stomach—but he turns away from you again, relax... finally he decides to walk towards you, so you tighten up your stomach again... and he steps very carefully over you, relax your stomach... now you decide to float up again into the air... your body is now floating towards school... see yourself floating into your school above everyone... no one sees you... but you can see everyone else... now you float into your classroom... you can see your teacher talking and you can see yourself and all the other students sitting at their seats... the teacher hands out a test... see yourself taking the test—you look so confident and relaxed—you're getting the answers correct... you're doing very well... you decide to leave since you see that you're doing so well on the test... let your body float back to the field, over the animals, back through the door into the dark room... as you float in the dark, you think about how proud you are of how well you were doing on your test... when you are ready slowly open your eyes.

Discuss how relaxed they feel and the importance of relaxing before a test. Suggest that they take their own "imaginary trip" before they take any test.

Closure: Ask the students to name other things they can do to help themselves do better on tests. Make a list on the board.

Getting Ready for a Test

Students should
draw themselves
in bed.

Students draw a nutritious
breakfast on the
plate.

GET A GOOD NIGHT'S SLEEP

EAT A WARM, NUTRITIOUS BREAKFAST

Students draw a
picture of themselves
doing what they do best
(ex: math, riding horses, etc.)

Students draw 2 pencils.

DO YOUR BEST

BRING 2 SHARPENED PENCILS

Students draw a clock and put the
hands on the clock (9:15)

Students draw a face with a smile
and big ears

BE PRESENT AND ON TIME
THE DAY OF THE TEST

BE A GOOD LISTENER DURING
THE TEST

Students draw two circles, each
about the size of a penny.

Students draw a picture of
themselves being real quiet
(tip-toeing, saying "Sh-h-h etc.)

COLOR ONE CIRCLE DARK AND ROUND
(stay within the circle)

BE REAL QUIET & DON'T
DISTURB OTHERS

Joe Wittmer, Ph.D. and Diane W. Thompson, M.Ed.

Activity 3.16

Ways I Work: A Self-Evaluation

Level:	Grades 3 to 10
Purpose:	To do a self evaluation related to one's study habits.
Materials:	"Self-Evaluation" worksheet copied for each student.
Activity:	Pass out the "Self-Evaluation" worksheet and then begin by saying: *Think about the activities on the worksheet and how you approach them. What are some of your positive (+) methods, or those ways that are productive, accomplish something for you, or are helpful? List these under the (+). What are some of your negative (-) methods or those ways that are not productive, interfere, or do not help you? List these under the (-).*
	Note: The students should do this individually and then share their responses in small groups, or as a class directed by you.
Closure:	Ask selected students to share their responses and lead a discussion on the positive and negative responses. Make a list on the board as the students share those previously written or as additional ones are generated from the discussion. Focus on how negative behaviors, if turned into positive behaviors, will help them become better students.

Self-Evaluation

This is what I do when I am:	POSITIVE	NEGATIVE
1. Reviewing for a test.	+	-
2. Listening to a lecture.	+	-
3. Watching a movie in school.	+	-
4. Doing homework.	+	-
5. Trying to get a good grade.	+	-
6. Doing a report.	+	-

Joe Wittmer, Ph.D. and Diane W. Thompson, M.Ed.

SECTION IV
DECISION MAKING

People must continually make decisions. The myriad of alternatives now available in our society has created a situation which causes many people, especially younger people, to be confused and to struggle in their attempts to make self-enhancing, productive decisions. The relatively stable social norms of the past in our country are in a state of transition, and as noted, in confusion, and flux. We live in a "micro-wave" society that often calls for quick, spontaneous, responsible decisions on the spur of the moment. Therefore, decision making has become much more complex and requires more skill, time, and energy than heretofore in our society.

All people are ultimately responsible for their lives. They create and shape their own present and future through decisions and choices they consciously or unconsciously make each day. Assuming personal responsibility for decisions we make is the "bottom line" in the decision-making process.

Examining the alternatives and the consequences surrounding any decision is, perhaps, the most crucial step in making a decision. There are a number of approaches which can be used to heighten students' awareness in the decision-making process. One method is to discourage the use of the words, "I can't..." and replace them with the phrase, "I choose not to, at this point in my life." This tends to emphasize the reality that there are alternatives available. Students see themselves as responsible for what happens in their lives. They sense more of their own "personal power" and realize that they have numerous opportunities to shape and brighten their own lives if only they choose to use the power available to them as human beings in a free society. Empowering them to make decisions is important.

Decision making involves the use of both our cognitive and effective domains and both are involved in determining the choices we make. Yet, many stress only the cognitive aspects and ignore or overlook the feelings that influence a decision. It is important to realize that each decision, whether appropriate or inappropriate, involves our feelings and that each decision we make influences us emotionally, and usually others, in the same manner. Questions such as "How would you feel if that happened?" or "How are you feeling as we talk about this decision you are about to make?" can assist us to see that there is a distinct relationship between thinking, feeling, and behavior. Many psychologists believe that our thinking determines our feelings which impact on our perceptions [our reality] at that moment. And further, that feelings and perceptions usually dictate how we behave in a particular situation.

One interesting and thought-provoking way to begin looking at the decision-making process is to have the students discuss their personal reactions to this quote: "Not to make a decision is a decision." A good class discussion will usually follow. As someone once said, "The greatest mistake we can make is to continually fear that we will make one." Many of the everyday decisions we make entail risks.

The activities in this section cover a wide range of topics—from selecting our peers, decisions about future careers, drug use, and personal decisions about life in general.

Joe Wittmer, Ph.D. and Diane W. Thompson, M.Ed.

Activity 4.1

Peer Pressure: How to Handle It Without Being a Geek

Level: Grades 7 to 10

Purpose: To help students recognize peer pressure situations and how to appropriately deal with such pressure, how to resolve peer pressure situations and to feel "OK" with the solution(s).

Materials: Students will need paper and pencil. Have copies of the 5 "Conflict Situations" available or on a transparency.

Activity: Begin by saying: *You are at that time in your life when friends are very important. You are beginning to become more independent from your parents and you are forming more complex and lasting relationships with your peers. Due to this independence, you are faced with more choices, many of which are very important to you currently as well as your future. Peers can have a strong influence on those choices.* Let them know that it is helpful to be aware that when conflict situations arise it is important to know how to respond to them in positive ways. *Often our peers pressure us to behave in certain ways. We want to feel good about the decisions that we make.*

Next, divide the class into five groups and ask each to select a leader/writer. Say: *Your task is to write out a situation involving negative peer pressure. Each group will receive a different topic. Write your situation from the topic (one of five). That is, stay on task. Do not write a solution, just the conflict situation. You will have approximately 10 minutes to write your situation. You will be trading your written conflict situation with another group, so be sure it is readable.*

Hand out a topic (or use overhead transparency) to each group and give them sufficient time to complete the task.

When the groups have finished the writing task, have each group read their conflict situation. Collect the situations and distribute the situations to different groups. Your task will be to discuss among yourselves how you will act out the conflict. *You will have two to three minutes to act out your situation. Keep in mind that you must come up with alternatives to the pressure instead of going along with the group.*

Allow approximately five minutes for the groups' discussions. Then have each group, in turn, role play or act out their solution to the situation.

Closure: Ask the class about other situations involving peer pressure, i.e., some examples not covered today. Then, lead a discussion on which of the role played "responses" was the most effective and why. You might close by saying: *Today you have delved into some of the conflict situations that can arise from peer pressure. The first step in resolving conflict is to be aware of the conflict situation. We have seen today that it is helpful to be aware of possible positive responses to conflict situations involving peer pressure. Even though our peers can pressure us to make negative choices, we do have the ultimate decision and we have to look at the consequences of those choices. We are the responsible ones. We choose our actions. No one can make us do anything we don't want to do. So, the next time you feel pressured to go along with the group when you wish not to, stop and think about some of the responses you learned today and how you might make them without feeling like a geek.*

Peer Conflict Situations

TOPIC #1

SHOPLIFTING

TOPIC #2

A FINAL EXAM HAS BEEN STOLEN AND THE TEACHER IS UNAWARE.

TOPIC #3

DRINKING ALCOHOL

TOPIC #4

USE OF ILLEGAL DRUGS

TOPIC #5

A BOY/GIRL RELATIONSHIP GONE BAD

Joe Wittmer, Ph.D. and Diane W. Thompson, M.Ed.

Activity 4.2

If You Don't Know Where You're Going, You'll Probably End Up Somewhere Else*

Level:	Grades 6 to 12
Purpose:	To help students identify personal goals and to become aware of the importance of planning ahead.
Materials:	Transparency and overhead or chalkboard. "Rating Future Goals" activity sheet for each student (or as a transparency, or place on chalkboard).
Activity:	You might say: *All the things you've just imagined in your perfect day might be considered the same as your life goals. A goal is anything you want or need. How do you make sure you get the things you want?* (Elicit responses). *Yes, you plan for them. You set goals.*

Now, you might say: *Put your head on your desk, close your eyes, and imagine your perfect day. Think about:*

a. *Where you are in your "perfect day." (pause)?*

b. *Whom you are with? (pause)*

c. *What possessions you own: a car? A boat? (pause).*

d. *What kind of job you have? (pause)*

e. *What you are doing at the moment?*

Hold a discussion concerning the "perfect day." Elicit responses. Many student goals will be unrealistic, but that's OK. Tell them that shortly they'll be focusing on realistic goals concerning school and the future.

Next, pass out copies of the "Rating Future Goals." You might say: *Here are some possible goals for school and the future. Rate them according to their importance to you. Then choose from the listed goals the most important school goals and the most important future goals. If your most important goals are not on the list, write them in. Finally, write two realistic ways to reach each of your most important goals.*

Divide the class into triads and allow 10 minutes for the triad members to each share school and one future goal along with plans to meet their goals.

Closure:	Elicit students' responses by leading a discussion with the whole group concerning their most important goals and the steps one might take to reach them. Ask: *Will your goals stay the same? When and why might your goals change?* You might close by stating the following (in your own words): *Some things are fun to do on the "spur of the moment." However, many of the really important things in our lives require planning ahead and good decision making skills. To get what we want and need in our lives, it is necessary to decide on special goals and take steps to reach them. Keep in mind, just as the world around us is constantly changing, our goals may also change. What is important to remember is that if we want to reach our goals, we must plan ahead.*

*Adapted from, *IMPACT,* (1992). Orlando, FL. Orange County School System.

| Optional Assignment: | Ask the students to decide something they want or need this week and to set a goal and outline their steps to accomplish the goal. |

Rating Future Goals

Very Important	Somewhat Important	Not Important	
❏	❏	❏	1. Get along well with friends
❏	❏	❏	2 Get a college degree
❏	❏	❏	3 Get very high grades
❏	❏	❏	4. Accomplish what my parents feel I am capable of
❏	❏	❏	5. Be a good athlete
❏	❏	❏	6. Be a student leader
❏	❏	❏	7. Make a contribution to society
❏	❏	❏	8. Make a name for myself in my career
❏	❏	❏	9. Be able to help others
❏	❏	❏	10. Have a responsible job
❏	❏	❏	11. Be able to pursue my own interests in a creative way
❏	❏	❏	12. Lead an exciting, adventurous life
❏	❏	❏	13. Get married and have a nice family
❏	❏	❏	14. Make lots of money
❏	❏	❏	15. Have a steady, good-paying job that will last
❏	❏	❏	16. Other

To share during the triad experience:

My most important school goal is:　　1. _____

The best way to reach this goal is:　　_____

My most important future goal is:　　2. _____

The best way to reach this goal is:　　_____

I made these decisions because:　　3. _____

_____

Activity 4.3

If I Were King....

Level:

Grades 3 to 10

Purpose:

To provide students the opportunity to experience the power of making changes in their world with a magic wand, any changes they desire, the opportunity to share those with others, and to experience a joint decision-making process with fellow students.

Materials:

A copy of "The Magic Wand" worksheet for each student.

Activity:

Pass out the worksheets and allow time for the students to complete them. Then divide the class into triads and give them a few minutes to discuss their worksheet responses. Next, ask each triad to choose 5 of the 10 statements on the worksheet and give them 15 minutes to agree on the 5 incomplete sentence completions. Their assignment is to come to an agreement; no minority opinions permitted. That is, the three of them now have equal power in their kingdom! After 15 minutes, allow each triad to share with the larger group their joint, agreed to decisions and to then give their decision-making process.

Closure:

Look for general themes in the changes the different triads have decided to make in their world and lead a discussion on how their changes would change the world. Ask them to describe the world they have created. Is it a better world? A fair world? A good for everybody world?

The Magic Wand

1. I would alter _____

   _____

2. I would choose a new _____

   _____

3. I would never allow _____

   _____

4. I would always make _____

   _____

5. I would invent a _____

   _____

6. I would continue _____

   _____

7. I would stop _____

   _____

8. I would replace _____

   _____

Joe Wittmer, Ph.D. and Diane W. Thompson, M.Ed.

Activity 4.4

Pressure, Pressure, and More Pressure

Level:
Grades 5 to 8

Purpose:
To help students understand the effects of peer pressure on decision making.

Materials:
Duplicate copies of the "Pressure Seat Situations" (Select five for each group).

Activity:
Begin by saying: *All of us are faced with situations when our friends or acquaintances invite us to do whatever they are doing. Some of these things are good for us and some can be harmful to us. We all want to have friends. We sometimes feel pressure to join the crowd and to do whatever they are doing.*

Next, divide the students into groups of five. *Let's play a game called "Pressure Seat."* Select one student in each group to choose a pressure seat situation of the five given to each group. The student will read the situation aloud and respond in one minute. The group will discuss the situation and tell if they agree or disagree with the decision made by the student. The student in the pressure seat then chooses another to take his or her place. This student selects from the remaining four situations given the group and so on until each member of the group has been in the pressure seat.

Closure:
Conduct a discussion with the entire class and then ask: *How do you feel about the decisions you made? What are some of the factors you considered in making your decision? Some examples may be: peer pressure, consequences, and so forth. Peer pressure is part of everyday life. Being aware of the effects of peer pressure will help you make better decisions. Be aware of the effects peer pressure has on your daily decisions.*

Pressure Seat Situations

- You are on your way home from school. Your best friend shows you a pack of cigarettes and says, "Let's go over behind the building and smoke one." What would you do? Why?

- You are at school taking a test. The person sitting next you is cheating and offers the test answers to you. What would you do? Why?

- Three people in your room are wearing the most popular brand of athletic shoe. You really would like to have a pair and think your friends are cool. Your mother tells you she does not have the money to buy a pair. What would you do? Why?

- You are at your friend's house on Saturday. Your friend shows you a marijuana joint and tries to get you to smoke with him. What would you do? Why?

- Your friends decide they are mad at the teacher and are not going to study for the social studies test. They also are not going to do homework for the rest of the year. What would you do? Why?

- You are walking to school. Your friend, who often skips school, tries to get you to join him for a day of fun. What would you do? Why?

- You are going to the store for your mother and you see two of your older friends hanging around the store. They try to get you to steal a bag of chips for them and promise you a ride on their motorcycle in return. What would you do? Why?

- It is after dark and you are still playing outside. Some of your friends decide it would be fun to throw rocks at some cars. They want you to come along. What would you do? Why?

- All of your friends have a special girlfriend or boyfriend, it seems. You feel left out. You really don't want to have a "special friend" but several good friends. What would you do? Why?

- You've learned that another student has brought a gun to school. What would you do? Why?

- You are at home alone. Your mother has told you not to leave the house while she is gone. Your friend calls and wants you to come over and tells you that your mother will never know. What would you do? Why?

- You have permission to go skating with a friend. You are to be home by 9:00 p.m. Your friend decides to go next door for a hamburger after skating and wants you to go along. You realize that if you go along, you'll be late getting home. What would you do? Why?

- Your friend is passing notes in class which say ugly things about a classmate. Someone gives the note to you. What would you do? Why?

- Several of your friends are wearing makeup. Your parents think you are too young to wear makeup. What would you do? Why?

- Some of your friends have dyed their hair in a punk style. You really don't think it looks good, but would really like to feel more a part of the group. Your parents do not approve of punk hair styles. What would you do? Why?

- You are invited to a friend's house for a party. You get there and realize your friend's parents are not there. Your friend is drinking beer and offers you some. What would you do? Why?

- One of the students in your room tells you that if you don't want to get beaten up after school, you had better give him your lunch money. What would you do? Why?

Joe Wittmer, Ph.D. and Diane W. Thompson, M.Ed.

Activity 4.5

The Creative Experience

Level:	Grades 2 to 6
Purpose:	To develop creativity, stimulate the imagination, and create a decision-making situation.
Materials:	None.
Activity:	You might tape record the following fantasy. However, the script can also be read to the students. Regardless, speak softly, slowly, distinctly, and in a soothing voice. Whether you tape and then play it, or read it aloud, including soft music in the background can be helpful.

Ask everyone to close their eyes and to keep them closed until the voice on the tape (or you) says to open them. Play the tape (or read the following script):

The Experience

OK, now that your eyes are closed, get in the most comfortable position you can find. Put your hands and your feet where they are the most comfortable and relax. As I talk to you, imagine that with each and every breath you are becoming more and more relaxed. Now, rest your head, take a deep breath (pause) and hear my words. Listen. Let any noises around you just fade away....

All that is important now is that you relax. Just let yourself go, sink down (pause). Keep breathing deeply—in and out. Now, here in this very comfortable position, feeling very pleasant, imagine that your whole body has gone limp. Let any tension that you have in your body drain downward, down through your legs and out to the floor. You feel very loose, now, very tranquil. The feeling of looseness is all around you, peaceful, very calm and relaxed. You find yourself becoming even more and more relaxed now with each and every breath.

It's a warm, sunny day and you see a very beautiful field and you are walking barefoot across it toward a small woods off in the distance (pause). As you approach the woods, you can see the leaves on the trees and you can feel the green soft grass between your toes. There is a slight breeze... it brushes gently against your face. It's very pleasant. It feels so good to be so close to nature.

Slowly walking on, you come to the top of a small hill on the edge of the woods. You are standing in the grass. The grass is very green, soft like velvet to your feet... so delicate, so very soft and very delicate. You can feel it as it touches your feet (pause). You see beautiful flowers in bloom and smell their fragrances.

As you stand here on this small hill, looking out, you notice a small stream in front of you. The water is rippling slowly over some small stones in the stream and you can see the mist as it rises gently and slowly from the water. It is a beautiful sight and you're feeling so happy and pleasant.

Now, move away from the stream and walk back toward the woods. You can see the trees. Each tree becomes more and more vivid as you become more and more relaxed.... As you walk alone here in the woods, think about how beautiful and peaceful it is, how good it is to be this close to nature.

As you walk on you see the shadows of the trees cast on the ground below. You look up and see the sun twinkling through the trees (pause). *So peaceful. You walk on now and you come to a clearing at the end of the woods. There before you is a pond. The water is clear, so clear and quiet. It's not moving at all. It is like a mirror and you can see the reflections of the trees in the water* (pause). *You stop beside the pond, look down and put your hand in the water.... You can now feel the water on your hand.*

Take your hand out of water and gaze into this beautiful, clear pond. You begin to see your own reflection. It is becoming very clear now. You can see yourself. You are smiling. You can see what you are wearing. You are very relaxed (pause for 5 to 10 seconds). *Now, move away from the pond and walk across the beautiful field. In front of you there is a small mountain. As you gaze at the mountain you notice an opening—an opening in the side of the mountain leading into a cave* (pause).

You decide to go into the cave. As you enter the cave, you can see the rock formations, feel the moistness and in the background you can hear the drip, drip of water. The cave gradually leads down deeper into the ground. It is very quiet and peaceful here in the cave (pause). *You make your way down deeper into the cave. You stop to take a breath and relax. You are relaxing more with every moment, every breath... every passing moment... relaxing more. It is so quiet and peaceful here. You look there toward the back of the cave and notice a bright light coming from an opening at the back of the cave. You make your way through this opening now, going into another section of the cave. It is brightly lighted and it is a very beautiful area of the cave* (pause). *There in front of you is a statue. A statue* (pause). *Suddenly, you are aware that this statue can talk and is talking to you. Listen to what the statue says. Talk to the statue now.*

(Allow at least two minutes here. If you use music, let it play on.) *Now, I am going to ask you to make a decision concerning the statue. Will you bring the statue out with you, or will you leave it behind in the cave? You must decide now. You have just a moment.* (Pause for about 60 seconds.) *Okay, make your way back out of the cave, out into the sunlight* (pause).

Now, at the count of three you will open your eyes and you will feel alert and refreshed. One, two, you're becoming more alert. Three, gently stretch and open your eyes.

Joe Wittmer, Ph.D. and Diane W. Thompson, M.Ed.

After you've completed the reading (or tape playing), give the students ample opportunity to discuss their experiences. Be certain that all students get an opportunity, if desired, to tell their experiences. If you have a large class, you might break them up into small groups or triads for discussion. The discussion following an activity, where each student is facilitated to disclose feelings and ideas concerning the experience, is a significant aspect of this activity. No judging, interpreting, or advising should be permitted by anyone.

Next, lead a discussion concerning how the students decided whether to bring the statue out or leave it behind in the cave? Why? What were the deciding factors? How did they make the decision? Some children and adults see statues of themselves. It is common for adults to see Jesus or the Virgin Mary. Others see their parents or a favorite relative. The statue of David is also a favorite among adults. Perhaps this is because they are well-known statues and people are familiar with them, a reference point in which to project their fantasy. Discussions following the guided fantasy provide an opportunity to facilitate open, honest communication in atmosphere where facilitative conditions can be developed.

Closure: Close with a discussion on how students might use structured imagination to make decisions in their own lives. Sometimes it helps to simply lie down, relax, close your eyes, and "work through" or daydream a positive solution to difficult decision-making situations.

Activity 4.6

Nasty River

Level:	Grades 3 to 9
Purpose:	To help students recognize that people have varied values which affect and determine the way they behave and make decisions.
Materials:	"Nasty River Story," props and scrap paper.
Activity I:	Begin by telling the class to imagine that they are standing between a McDonalds and a Burger King. Get a show of hands on how many would choose McDonalds and how many would choose Burger King. Make a chart on the board under the headings of BURGER KING and McDONALDS.

Next, have the students share aloud their reasons for choosing one restaurant or the other and list them in the appropriate column. (Examples: good food, fun playground, cheap, nice people, etc.) After the list is complete, say something like: *How did you decide between the two restaurants? All of us make a lot of decisions each day and these decisions are based on things that are important to us. That is, we make personal decisions based on these 'things." These "things" that are important to us are called what? Who can tell me what they're called?* (Usually one or two students will know they're called values.)

Activity II: Have five students act out the "Nasty River" story as you read it aloud. Tell the rest of the class to watch carefully because they are going to have to decide who is the worst (most mean, most slimy, etc.) least desirable character in the story. (It is helpful to have props for the characters, e.g., slugger with a baseball bat.)

Then, have the students rank order the characters from the least desirable to the most desirable friend (in their view) on a slip of paper.

Next, take a class vote on who is the least desirable character in the story. Have the students discuss their reasons for the character they select.

An alternative is to develop scripts and have selected class members role-play the characters.

Closure: Ask the students to share their reasons for their decisions and what personal values their reasons reflect. For example, if they felt that Sinbad is the least desirable because he is violent, they then value non-violence, peace and calm ways to express anger. Other values expressed might be honesty, friendship, kindness, helpfulness, and so forth.

Ask two or three volunteers to sum up in one sentence what they learned about the relationship between "values" and "decisions." You might end with a statement like: *As you can see from our discussion today, people have different values. And these values affect the way you and others make decisions. What type of values do you hold? Are they viewed by others as good or bad?*

Joe Wittmer, Ph.D. and Diane W. Thompson, M.Ed.

Nasty River

Once there was a girl named Abigail who was in love with a boy named Gregory. Gregory had an unfortunate mishap and broke his glasses. Abigail, being a true friend, volunteered to take them to be repaired. But the repair shop was across the river, and during a flash flood the bridge was washed away. Poor Gregory could see nothing without his glasses, so Abigail was desperate to get across the river to the repair shop. While she was standing forlornly on the bank of the river, clutching the broken glasses in her hands, a boy named Sinbad glided by in a rowboat.

She asked Sinbad if he would take her across. He agreed to on condition that while she was having the glasses repaired, she would go to a nearby store and steal a transistor radio that he had been wanting. Abigail refused to do this and went to a friend named Ivan who had a boat.

When Abigail told Ivan her problem, he said he was too busy to help her out and didn't want to be involved. Abigail, feeling that she had no other choice, returned to Sinbad and told him she would agree to his plan.

When Abigail returned the repaired glasses to Gregory, she told him what she had to do. Gregory was appalled at what she had done and told her he never wanted to see her again.

Abigail, upset, turned to Sinbad with her tale of woe. Sinbad was so sorry for Abigail that he promised her he would get even with Gregory. They went to the school playground where Gregory was playing ball and Abigail watched while Sinbad beat Gregory up and broke his glasses again.

Activity 4.7

Vandalism

Level:	Grades 5 to 9
Purpose:	To have students think about the impact of vandalism and to voice their opinions concerning the victims, the resulting property damage, and the role parents should or should not play in making restitution.
Materials:	Copies of "What Do You Think?" handout for each participant.
Activity:	You might begin by saying: *Sometimes some teenagers start fooling around. The fooling around becomes destructive. They end up wrecking and destroying property that does not belong to them."*

This is called vandalism. The amount of vandalism by teenagers is rising. Some cities and towns now make parents pay for the damage done by their children.

Do you think this is right? The handouts list some opinions on the subject. Mark those with which you agree with an "x" and write "no" next to those items with which you disagree. Then write your opinion at the end.

Next, divide the class into small groups, appoint a leader for each group, and have them discuss their "What Do You Think?" responses and to be prepared to give a brief report to the larger group concerning the general consensus, if any, of their specific group.

Closure:	

Close by having each small group leader make a brief report to the larger group. Then, discuss problems at your school or community in terms of vandalism that has occurred. Selected students written opinions can be discussed and shared among the entire group.

Joe Wittmer, Ph.D. and Diane W. Thompson, M.Ed.

What Do You Think?

Read each statement below and place an "x" beside each item with which you agree and write "no" next to the item with which you disagree. Be prepared to discuss your decisions.

_____1. Many parents don't know what their kids are up to. I think it's a good idea to make them pay for any damage their children do. Then they would keep track of their children.

_____2. No one should have to pay for damage caused by someone else. Parents can't control everything their kids do. It isn't fair to make them pay the price.

_____3. Teenagers say they want to be treated like grown-ups. Well, grown-ups who break the law must pay fines or go to jail. Teenagers should be treated the same way.

_____4. I don't think parents should have to pay for their children's vandalism. If they do, they might get really angry at their kids. Then the kids, feeling angry, might go out and destroy more property. They might do this to "get back at" their parents.

_____5. But what about the victims of vandalism? Suppose you own a shop, and some kids break all the windows. Or suppose some kids paint their names all over your car. Shouldn't you be paid for the damage? I think the kids should have to pay you. And if they can't, their parents should.

_____6. This is unfair to parents who are poor. Where are they going to get money to pay for damage caused by their kids?

_____7. But this might stop some kids from destroying property. If you know your parents couldn't pay for damage, you probably wouldn't destroy things.

_____8. I don't think a kid throwing a rock through a window expects to get caught. And he is not going to stop and wonder if his parents can pay the fine.

_____9. When kids destroy property, they alone should pay for it. Otherwise, they won't learn their lesson. A friend of mine couldn't care less if she costs her parents money. When she cracked up the family car, she just shrugged it off.

_____10. I think its okay for parents to pay for damage their children do. But their kids should do some paying, too. They could pay back their parents by working. Or they could do free work for the person whose property they damaged.

_____11. The answer is to have a curfew for teens—10 p.m. weekdays and midnight weekends.

Your opinion: _____

_____

_____

Activity 4.8

Forced Choices

(May require two sessions)

Level:	Grades 3 to 6
Purpose:	To practice ranking alternatives in order to learn their importance in making better choices.
Materials:	"Rank Order: A Forced Choice" (copies for everyone).
Activity:	Review with the students every day decision making and how we go about making these choices. Talk about how we often rank our alternatives in order to make better choices.
	Give the students a copy of the worksheet. Ask them to rank order the choices for each question as best they can. Ask that each choice be ranked.
Closure:	Discuss one question at a time and have the students give reasons for their personal rank order. That is, how did they decide the ranking for a particular item? How do our decisions coincide with out values? Have the class decide on a new question (one they feel was left off the list) and then write three different answers for it. The students should then rank their choices individually.

Rank Order: A Forced Choice

(Rank order each set with #1 being your first choice. Do not leave any items unranked)

1. Which do you least like to do?
   ____ get up in the morning
   ____ go to bed at night
   ____ keep your room neat

2. Which kind of teacher do you prefer?
   ____ a nasty person but a good teacher
   ____ a nice person but a poor teacher
   ____ personality and teaching ability about average

3. Which would you prefer to do?
   ____ do better in school
   ____ make a new friend
   ____ go on a long vacation

4. Which chore would you rather do?
   ____ wash dishes
   ____ dust the furniture
   ____ take the garbage out

5. What would you do if someone hit you?
   ____ tell the teacher or someone else at school
   ____ hit him/her back
   ____ walk away

6. Which would you least like to do?
   ____ move to a new school
   ____ lose your wallet
   ____ break a leg

7. Would you rather be the...
   ____ mother
   ____ father
   ____ baby in the family

8. What kind of person do you least like to sit next to? Someone who...
   ____ talks a lot
   ____ looks at your paper
   ____ can't sit still and bothers you

9. How would you rather be punished?
   ____ spanking
   ____ by taking away TV privileges
   ____ by talking to you
   ____ time out to your room

10. What is hardest for you to do?
    ____ be quiet
    ____ talk in front of the group
    ____ talk to the teacher

11. Which do you like least?
    ____ a classmate who plays practical jokes on you
    ____ a classmate who constantly tattles
    ____ a classmate who gossips about other people

12. To whom would you tell a secret?
    ____ your friend
    ____ your teacher
    ____ your parent
    ____ your school counselor

13. What would you like to do least?
    ____ report someone who is sexually harassing you
    ____ forget the harassment
    ____ confront the person doing the harassing

14. What would you do if you knew a friend shoplifted?
    ____ report him/her
    ____ pretend you didn't see
    ____ ask him/her to share it with you or you would report it

15. Which would be hardest for you to do?
    ____ show a bad paper to your parents
    ____ walk away from a fight
    ____ wait your turn when you have something exciting to say

16. Which of these would you most likely do if you knew someone had brought a gun to school?
    ____ report him/her to the police
    ____ report him/her to a school teacher or other school authority
    ____ do nothing

17. Which would make you most uneasy?
    ____ a young blind person
    ____ a young disabled person
    ____ a person from a different race
    ____ someone of your race

18. Which would make you most uneasy?
    ____ a thunderstorm
    ____ knowing someone was gossiping about you
    ____ knowing someone who is being abused by his or her parents

Activity 4.9

Making More Choices

(May require two sessions)

Level:	Grades 6 to 12
Purpose:	To provide the opportunity to choose among alternatives that require thoughtful consideration and decision making.
Materials:	"Rank Order" exercise sheet for each participant, pencils.
Activity:	Pass out a "Rank Order" sheet to each participant. Explain to the group that they will be responding to questions that will require them to look deeper into themselves and make a value judgment-type decision. There will be three or four responses to each question. Each person is to rank the order of responses according to his or her own value-laden preferences. They should not leave any unranked.
Closure:	To process the exercise you may ask the group which questions they would like to talk about and then lead a discussion around the following:

a. Which questions were most difficult? Why?

b. What personal value does that particular question indicate?

c. Were there right or wrong decisions?

d. What do you know about your friends' values, parents' values, and so forth regarding a specific question?

Rank Order

Rank order each set with #1 being your first choice.

1. Which is most important in a friendship?
   ____ loyalty
   ____ generosity
   ____ honesty
   ____ money

2. Which season do you like best?
   ____ winter
   ____ summer
   ____ spring
   ____ fall

3. If you won the million dollar lotto, what would you do with it?
   ____ save it
   ____ give 10% of it to charity
   ____ buy something for yourself-cars, a boat, and so forth
   ____ buy a new house for your parents

4. Which do you think is most harmful?
   ____ cigarettes
   ____ marijuana
   ____ alcohol

5. How late should students your age be allowed to stay out on a weekend night?
   ____ 10 p.m.
   ____ midnight
   ____ it's up to them

6. If you were a parent, by what time would you expect a person your age to be home?
   ____ 10 p.m.
   ____ 12 p.m.
   ____ it's up to him or her

7. Where would you prefer to live?
   ____ on a farm
   ____ in the suburbs
   ____ in an inner city

8. Which do you like best?
   ____ winter in the mountains
   ____ summer by the sea
   ____ autumn in the country

9. Which would you rather be?
   ____ an only child
   ____ the youngest child
   ____ the oldest child

10. Which pet would you prefer?
    ____ a cat
    ____ a dog
    ____ a turtle
    ____ a parakeet

11. If you were president, to which would you give the highest priority?
    ____ space program
    ____ poverty program
    ____ defense program
    ____ the national debt
    ____ health car

12. Which would you least like to be?
    ____ very poor
    ____ very sickly
    ____ disfigured

13. Whom would you prefer to marry? A person with
    ____ intelligence
    ____ personality
    ____ sex appeal
    ____ lots of money

14. For which do you think more money should be spent?
    ____ space launches
    ____ slum clearance
    ____ a cure for cancer

15. What would you be most likely to do about a person who had bad breath?

_____ directly tell him or her

_____ send him or her anonymous note

_____ nothing

16. Which would you prefer to have happen to you if you had bad breath?

_____ be told directly

_____ receive an anonymous note

_____ not be told

17. When you worry about your grade on an exam, do you think about?

_____ yourself

_____ your parents

_____ pleasing the teacher

_____ getting into college

18. Which type of teacher do you most prefer?

_____ strict in the classroom but little homework

_____ strict in the classroom and much homework

_____ easy-going in the classroom but much homework

19. Which would you most like to improve?

_____ your looks

_____ your self-esteem

_____ the way you use your time

_____ your social life

20. Which would you least like to do?

_____ listen to a Beethoven symphony

_____ watch a debate

_____ watch a Shakespearean play

21. How do you have the most fun?

_____ alone

_____ with a large group

_____ with a few friends

22. If you had $500 to spend on decorating this classroom, would you spend

_____ $500 for an original painting

_____ $400 on furniture and $100 for an original painting

_____ entire sum on furniture

23. Pretend you are married and have your own family. Your mother has died and your father is old. What would you do?

_____ invite him to live in your home

_____ place him in a home for the aged

_____ get him an apartment for himself

24. If your parents were in constant conflict, which would you rather have them do?

_____ divorce, and your father leave home

_____ stay together and hide their feelings for the sake of the children

_____ divorce, and you live with your father

_____ divorce, and you live with your mother

25. Which would you rather your sister give you for your birthday?

_____ $20 to buy something

_____ a $20 gift of her choice

_____ something she made for you

Joe Wittmer, Ph.D. and Diane W. Thompson, M.Ed.

Activity 4.10

Break an Egg

Level: Grades 3 to 12

Purpose: To practice solving a problem using a group decision-making process while choosing from several alternatives.

Materials: Raw eggs, paper clips, rubber bands, paper, masking tape, string, paper cups, and large manila envelopes.

Activity: Hold a raw egg up and ask the class what will happen if the egg is dropped in an empty trash can. (It will break.) Drop the egg into the trash can!

Tell the class that their goal for today's activity is to drop a raw egg from 10 feet (or whatever height) up and keep it from breaking.

Divide the class into groups of 4 or 5 members each. Give each group a manila envelope with several paper clips, rubber bands, a paper cup, a 4-foot piece of string, a pair of scissors and 3-foot pieces of masking tape. (You can add more items or vary the items, making sure each group has the same items.)

Tell each group to discuss several alternative ways to use the items found within the envelope to keep the egg from breaking when it is dropped. Their goal is to choose one of the methods proposed by their groups, discuss it, make a decision as a group, and then implement it.

Move the class outside to drop the eggs. Find some steps, a roof, or a step ladder from which each group, one at a time, drops their eggs.

Closure: Return inside and discuss the experience. Ask the following questions while allowing members from each group an opportunity to respond:

- *What did you experience while doing this activity?*
- *What was it like making a plan to solve a problem with a group?*
- *What were some of the problems your group had in solving the problem?*
- *How did you decide on the method used?*
- *How well did your group work together?*
- *How did your group choose which alternative to use to protect the egg?*

Activity 4.11

Good or Poor Decisions

Level: Grades 3 to 6

Purpose: To explore the decision-making process and to study the consequences of our decisions.

Materials: Paper, pencil/pen.

Activity: Give some examples of decisions students of this age are faced with and then ask them to do the following: *First, divide your piece of paper in half. Mark the top half of the page "Good Decisions." Mark the words "Poor Decisions" on the bottom section. Now, thinking back over some important decisions you have made during the past six months, categorize them according to the results* (of the decision you made) *in each case as either "good or poor." Write key words describing the decision in the appropriate section.* Next, ask them to look at the "Good Decisions" section and to ask themselves the following questions:

A. *How did I come to make these decisions?*

B. *Who was influential in my making the decision?*

C. *How many of these decisions were the result of my having received advice from others?*

Next, ask them to ask themselves these same questions as they look at the "Poor Decisions" section. Then, have them write down their impressions of this activity in regards to what they learned or relearned about themselves today.

Have the students pair off and discuss what they learned or relearned from the activity.

Closure: Remind the students to consider decisions that they have made at school, at home, in relation to their friends, at their job, and so forth. You may need to provide some examples in order to get them thinking and recalling. Lead a closing discussion on the following:

1. *How responsible are we for determining our futures? What about a person who is born into poverty? Or handicapped? Or who is a victim of abusive parents?*

2. *Do we have to give up our spontaneity in order to be responsible decision makers?*

Joe Wittmer, Ph.D. and Diane W. Thompson, M.Ed.

Activity 4.12
Making Your Choice

Level:	Grades 3 to 8
Materials:	"Your Choice" worksheet for each student.
Activity:	Place the students into small groups and then hand out the "Your Choice" worksheet and have each student choose the five most important decisions. Each group should tabulate the results to determine a group decision on their top five and then report their results to the larger group.
Closure:	Close with a discussion on the reasons for their choices. Focus on how our personal values enter into our decision-making process.

Your Choice

Making decisions are a part of your everyday experience. It is important to look at the problem and the consequences when deciding just what to do.

Gerardo had these decisions to make during his day. Choose the five most important decisions you feel he faced and tell why these would be important. Rank order your top five with the one listed first being your group's most important decision facing Gerardo. Use the democratic process in making your group's rankings.

1. To get out of bed.
2. To brush teeth and wash face or sleep longer.
3. Report someone who brought illegal drugs to school.
4. Whether to eat breakfast or meet the group early.
5. Talk with friends in front of school or look over notes for a math test first hour.
6. To cheat on math test or make it on his own.
7. To eat lunch at school or try to make it to Burger King without getting caught.
8. To ride the bus home or walk with friends.
9. To give his speech today or try to get out of it until tomorrow.
10. To play tennis after school or clean the garage as parents desire.
11. To go to a party Saturday night or to the baseball game with Dad.
12. To watch a special on TV or study for a science test being given the next day.
13. To report someone who has a gun in his or her locker.
14. Report a friend who he knows cheated on an exam.

Decision	Your Reason
# _____	_____
# _____	_____
# _____	_____
# _____	_____
# _____	_____

Joe Wittmer, Ph.D. and Diane W. Thompson, M.Ed.

Activity 4.13

A Decision-Making Model

Level:	Grades 9 to 12
Purpose:	To learn a method of structured decision making.
Materials:	Overhead projector, a copy of the "Decision Making Model" for all students, pencils, and a transparency of the model.
Activity:	Pass out copies of the model and begin by saying: *We all have to make decisions during the day. What are some of the decisions you have already made today?* (Elicit responses from the group.) *Today we are going to learn one process of decision making. There are other models available.* Next, explain the "Decision Making Model." Then, using the transparency, take the class through a decision-making situation using the model.
	Next, divide the class into four or five groups. Distribute one of the situation statements to each group. Ask the group to resolve the situation using the model. The recorder for each group writes the response. Allow each group 5 to 7 minutes to solve the problem.
	Have each group share their problem situation and their response to the entire class. Ask each group how they arrived at their response.
Closure:	Discuss the decisions made by each group. Then close by asking if this decision-making model can make decision making easier? Request they use the decision-making model sometime during this week.

Decision-Making Model

1. **Situation:**
   a. What is the problem?
   b. Who is concerned?
   c. When and where did it begin?

2. **Search For Possible Action Choices**

   Have you considered what action or actions you can take? Perhaps you might want to brainstorm these. Write down as many as you like, regardless of how different or impossible they seem. Do you think a teacher, a friend, your parents, or your school counselor might suggest some other ideas?

3. **Which Action Will Be Best For You?**
   (Consequences)
   a. Now what will be the results of each of your suggested actions?
   b. For each action, think what might possibly happen (negative and positive) if you follow through with such an idea. You might also want to write this down.

4. **Choosing The One Best Decision**

   Then make a choice keeping in mind how you feel about yourself, what's important to you, and what it might mean to you later. What consequences are you able to accept? Now that you've made your decision, let's act on it! What will you do?

5. **Will You be Satisfied With The Effect Of Your Decision**
   (Assessment of Decision)

   What would most likely happen? Would things go well? Would it be what you expected? Do you have good feelings about your results?

Joe Wittmer, Ph.D. and Diane W. Thompson, M.Ed.

Activity 4.14

Solving Problems Independently

Level: Grades 4 to 8

Materials: Transparency of A, B, C questions below.

Purpose: This activity provides practice in the decision-making process.

Activity: Place the A, B, C transparency on the overhead projector and read the twelve (12) situations given below (one at a time). Ask the following three questions (A,B,C) about each situation and write the students' responses on the board (or use a student volunteer). Discuss the students' answers to the three questions (A,B,C) before moving on to the next situation. (You might want to have students write their A-B-C responses to each situation.)

    A. *What could you do in this situation?*

    B. *Name as many ways to solve the problem as you can.*

    C. *What are the consequences of your actions?*

Situations:

1. Your teacher asks you to finish your work and you don't want to.
2. Your classmates tease you whenever you try to play kickball.
3. Your classmates have started a terrible untrue rumor about you.
4. Your friend tries to get you to shoplift.
5. Your teacher leaves the room and someone begins pushing you.
6. You are accused of taking money from a classmate and you didn't take the money.
7. You borrow a record from a friend and it gets broken.
8. You have a headache after lunch and you can't concentrate on your work.
9. Your classroom is too noisy and you are trying to do your work.
10. A friend refers to your mother in a very derogatory manner.
11. You know someone who brought drugs to school today.
12. You know someone who brought a weapon to school today.

Closure: Discuss what makes some personal decisions easier than others? Discussion should include: consequences, number of alternatives, and how it affects ourselves and others.

Activity 4.15

Setting Priorities

Level: Grades 9 to 12

Purpose: To practice the skill of decision making by becoming more aware of alternatives and personal values.

Materials: Copies of the questions (below) for each student.

Activity: Ask the students to look at each of the following rank ordered questions and to write a #1 to indicate their top priority, a #2 for their second priority and a #3 for their lowest priority:

A. What is the most important characteristic that your boy/girl friend can possess?

_____ good-looking

_____ fun at parties

_____ intelligent

_____ be wealthy

B. Where would you rather be on a Saturday afternoon?

_____ watching a sports program on TV

_____ at the beach

_____ on a picnic with your family

_____ drinking beer with friends

C. What is the one thing about school that you would really like to see changed?

_____ the grading system

_____ going five days a week

_____ the teachers

_____ the cafeteria food

D. Which would you "least" like to be?

_____ very poor

_____ confined to a wheelchair

_____ blind

_____ deaf

E. Which would you give up, if you had to?

_____ religious freedom

_____ economic freedom

_____ political freedom

Place the students into small groups, appoint leaders, and request they discuss their individual responses and how they arrived at their rankings.

More involvement might be generated by developing your own rank orders out of the issues which seem most relevant to your own local setting. For example, you could have the students rank order three qualities that they would value in choosing a college: a) located close to home; b) has a good reputation; c) the student/teacher ratio is very low. Or you could add a fourth and fifth alternative to each rank order and then have them set their priorities.

Closure:

In closing, conduct a discussion around the following:

1. *What priorities in your own life do you have the most difficulty in rank ordering?*

2. *What can you do to increase the probability that you will be aware of all of the alternatives available to you in any situation?*

3. *What are the three highest priorities in your life right now? How did you come to value these three over others?*

Things Aren't Always What They Seem

Level: Grades 1 to 5

Purpose: For students to understand that there are always two sides to every situation and that both should be evaluated before a decision is made.

Materials: Enlarged pictures of Illusions.

Activity: Begin by having the students put hand over one eye like a telescope and wink their eyes. Talk about how the image looks as if it's moving but it is not.

Next, show pictures of the Illusions. Talk about how people can see different things in the same picture. Relate this to how people can have a difference of opinion about what happened on the playground, cafeteria, and so forth as well.

Then have 5 students do a "role play" of students walking in line (all eyes toward the front) and the last one in line pushes (gently) and causes a chain reaction causing the first person in line to stumble slightly. (Be very careful with this activity.)

Then ask each one in the line who caused the problem. (Most students will blame the person directly behind them.) Who actually caused the problem? (The last person.) Next, have the students share examples of a time they were blamed for something that they did not do; and a time they blamed someone else for something that the person was not responsible for doing.

Closure: Ask 2 or 3 students to sum up what they learned from the activities today. Then discuss how it is best to objectively look at both sides before making a decision or taking sides. Also, discuss how one's "reality" is based on that person's perception. And, that there are as many "perceptions" of an event as there are people involved. End with a statement like: *It is important to look at all possibilities in a situation before you make a decision about what you should do. It is very important not to take sides in an issue until you've "worn the shoes" without criticism or judgment of all the people involved.*

Joe Wittmer, Ph.D. and Diane W. Thompson, M.Ed.

The Illusions

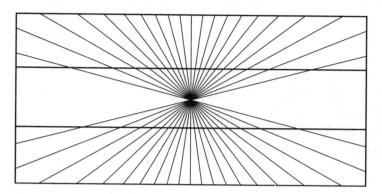

Are the lines all straight?

Do you see the profiles first or the goblet?

Can you see both women?

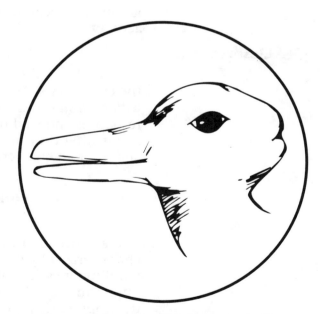

Do you see a rabbit or a duck

Activity 4.17

Using, Abusing, Enabling*

Level:
Grades 7 to 12

Purpose:
To develop an awareness of the symptoms of teenage substance abuse and to illustrate the roles others play in chemical dependency, and to eventually use this knowledge to make an informed decision regarding substance abuse.

Materials:
Transparency of "Symptoms of Teenage Substance Abuse" and "Enabling" worksheets or handouts for each student. Students also need pencil and paper. Have copies of the five enabling family member definitions on separate papers for each of the five groups.

Activity:
Begin by saying: *Substance abuse is the number one disease affecting teenagers today. With the availability of cocaine and alcohol in our area, teens who become users often become abusers almost overnight. In order to make intelligent decisions about the use of drugs and alcohol, we need to know what drug dependency is and what symptoms mark substance abuse.* Next, use a transparency or handout of "Symptoms of Teenage Substance Abuse" and "Enabling" for discussion by the class, then go over the role of the enabler and the effects on family members. Define enabler before moving on.

Divide the class into groups of 5 or 6 each (no more than 5 groups). Ask each group to write a situation taking one of the five roles of enabling family members (IP; CE; H; LC; M). Allow about 15 minutes for this activity.

Closure:

Have each group report its role (and the situation the group wrote) to the entire class. Ask: *What can we do as family members to help someone with a substance abuse problem rather than to enable them to continue?* Elicit responses and lead the discussion. Close by asking them to be thinking about what they might do if they were to identify someone as being an abuser or an enabler.

Symptoms of Teenage Substance Abuse

Adolescence is a time of change and development which may be characterized by periods of unusual behavior which is often justified as "finding oneself, being my own person, or finding where I fit." It is important to note that basically adolescence is a growing and developmental process, not a destructive and regressive period in one's life. Many of the following symptoms are, indeed, characteristic of "normal" adolescence. However, when you see a pattern or consistency of these symptoms, it would be well to investigate the possibility of chemical dependency.

*Adapted from, *IMPACT* (1992). Orlando, FL. Orange County Public Schools.

Joe Wittmer, Ph.D. and Diane W. Thompson, M.Ed.

Family

1. Changing attitudes toward rules and regulations.
2. Lack of participation in family activities.
3. Isolating, staying in room much of the time while at home.
4. Breaking curfew, sneaking out at night.
5. Stealing items from the home—money, pills, alcohol, and so forth
6. Lying—blaming others for troubles.

Friends

1. Sudden change in peer relationships.
2. Your friend is suddenly uncomfortable in your home with your parents there.

Schools

1. Grades fall.
2. Skips classes or entire days.
3. Sleeps in class.
4. Disrespectful to teachers.
5. Suspensions, expulsion.
6. Lack of motivation, lack of self-discipline.
7. Drops out of activities, and sports, and so forth.

Legal

1. Thefts, assaults, arrests.
2. DWI's
3. Speeds or drives recklessly.

Personal Health

1. Subtle change in personality, mood swings.
2. Weight loss/gain.
3. Erratic sleeping and eating habits.
4. Deep, nagging cough which persists.
5. Dilated pupils, eyes are red; uses eye drops or sunglasses.
6. Blackouts, short-term memory loss.
7. Hangovers.
8. Flashbacks.

Enabling

Enabling is to supply with the means, knowledge, or opportunity to be or do something; to make feasible or possible.

Enabling in the true sense of the definition means something positive, but when we consider the term as it relates to chemical dependency it has an entirely different meaning. Enabling is usually done with caring motives in an effort to help or fix the chemically dependent person. Because chemical dependency is a progressive illness, the person who is using chemicals experiences a deterioration of his or her ability to make responsible choices and must rely on others. The enabler unconsciously does not allow the chemically dependent person to suffer the consequences of his or her use.

Below is a list of attitudes and behaviors the enabler experiences:

1. Accepts the user's behavior and makes excuses for his or her dependency.
2. Covers up to protect work, school, and so forth.
3. Avoids problems—keeps the peace, believes that lack of conflict will solve the problems.
4. Minimizes. "Things aren't really that bad; it will get better when...."
5. Takes over the chemically dependent person's responsibilities.
6. Tries to control the chemically dependent person.
7. Endures. "This, too, shall pass."
8. Waits. "God will take care of it."

It is important to realize that chemically dependent people will continue to use and abuse unless they are allowed to suffer consequences. When we stop making excuses and bailing them out of trouble, they will have a much better chance of experiencing reality and seeking help for their problem.

Joe Wittmer, Ph.D. and Diane W. Thompson, M.Ed.

Roles

1. **Identified Patient (IP).** The chemically dependent person received a disproportionate amount of attention. This person is usually excused for being irresponsible due to being unable to cope with life's situations. The other family members pick up the slack and take over his or her responsibilities, and they do not allow the patient to suffer natural consequences from usage.

2. **Chief Enabler (CE).** This is any member of the family who takes the primary responsibility for the identified patient. This enabler usually believes that he or she has the power to fix the patient, and most of his or her energy is channeled in that direction.

3. **Hero (H).** This is the person who sets out to bring self-worth to the family. This is usually a very successful individual who has a high need for approval. The hero tries hard to fix things, and feels responsible for the family plan.

4. **Lost Child (LC).** This is the person who brings relief to the family. This is a quiet child who avoids stress at all cost. The lost child does not seek attention, either positive or negative, and has difficulty with intimate relationships.

5. **Mascot (M).** This is the person who sets out to ease tension in the family. Mascots are usually fun to be around, and they often use charm and humor to survive in the painful family system. This individual gets a lot of negative attention and he or she helps take the focus off the identified patient.

Activity 4.18

What Would You Do?*

Level:	Grades 6 to 12
Purpose:	To elicit decision-making responses to situations involving drug and alcohol use.
Materials:	Overhead or chalkboard. One Decision-Making Situation for each group. Students need pencil and paper.
Activity:	Divide the class into groups of 4 or 5 and appoint a leader for each. Hand each group leader one of the "Situations." Ask them to discuss their situation and answer the following four questions regarding it. (You may wish to make a transparency of these four questions.)

> 1. *What would you do in this situation?*
>
> 2. *How did you make that decision?*
>
> 3. *What should you do in that situation?*
>
> 4. *On what is your "should" based?*

Have the small groups read their situations and report their responses to the four questions to the entire group. Ask the large group as a whole for additional answers or ideas.

Closure:	You might close by saying: *Each individual must make his or her own decision about the use of chemical substances, but we all have a responsibility to see that use doesn't become abuse. Only if we are well-informed about the substances being offered can we make intelligent choices. Give some careful consideration to what you would really do when faced with a situation of substance abuse.*

*Adapted from, *IMPACT* (1992). Orlando, FL. Orange Country Public Schools

Decision Situations

SITUATION 1: Billy's locker is next to Dwight's. Everyone at school is hinting that Billy is a great party guy and can always provide something extra to drink, but Dwight can't believe things are really that bad. One day, though, he sees a bottle of bourbon in Billy's locker. He thinks about telling his school counselor or favorite teacher, but he doesn't want to be a "nerd."

SITUATION 2: Jeremy sometimes smokes pot and drinks beer at parties. He believes he is in control and can quit anytime he wants. As Jeremy's best friend, you've noticed that the partying has moved from Saturday to Friday and now sometimes begins right after school. You're afraid the drinking and drugs have taken control.

SITUATION 3: Janine is filling out an application for a part-time job and comes to the question, "Have you ever used drugs?" She did in the past, but went to a rehabilitation center and has been straight for over a year. If she answers "no," she will be lying, but if she answers "yes," she probably will not get the job which she really needs.

SITUATION 4: You're at a party given by a group you've wanted to belong to for a long time. They're the most popular crowd at school and being accepted by them means no more struggling to be noticed. Just as you begin to have a really good time, the host brings out some pot and starts to pass it around. You've promised your parents that you'll never use drugs, but refusing means that you'll never be part of the group.

SITUATION 5: You're taking the shortcut home after school. Just as you come around the corner of the gym, you see two boys exchanging pills and money. Jack Jock is the captain of the football team and the most popular boy in school. You're sure he's buying drugs from the school dealer. Jack is everyone's idol and you're sure no one will believe you if you say he's on drugs.

Activity 4.19

The Volunteer Experience

Level: Grades 3 to 7

Purpose: To help students realize some of the inner conflicts involved in decision making.

Materials: A copy of the "Experience" to read aloud.

Activity: Begin by asking for some volunteers. However, don't tell them what you want the volunteers to do; rather, make it a little mysterious, perhaps emphasizing that it will be challenging. Take a little time to let the suspense build, before saying: *Okay, Stop Thinking Now about whether or not you want to volunteer!* Next, place them into groups of 4 or 5 each. Ask them to close their eyes and to be quiet and listen carefully while you read the following:

The Experience

Make yourself as comfortable as you can and close your eyes. Take a deep breath and relax.

Now that your eyes are closed, I want you to focus on the experience you've just had. I just asked for some volunteers and each of you had to decide what to do. Should you volunteer or not? Now, imagine that there are two people in your head, one arguing that you should volunteer and the other arguing against it.

Listen to their arguments for a minute, as each tries to convince you what to do. (pause)

Now, let them continue trying to convince you, but this time they are not talking. What are they doing? How are they trying to convince you what to do? Watch them. (pause)

Now, they stop and leave you to make your own decision. (pause) *OK, open your eyes.*

Then say: *You see, I really didn't need any volunteers. I wanted you to think about the arguments that would be used to influence your actions. What happened when I asked you to let the two people argue and try to convince you what to do ? How did their voices sound? How were they dressed? Was one bigger than the other? What happened when they didn't use spoken words. How did they try to convince you? Who was winning when I asked you to stop? Discuss these questions within your group.*

Closure: Close by having each group give a summary of the major points made in their group. Ask them if they can see how this "goes on" within their respective heads each time they are in a situation where a decision needs to be made. Close with a discussion on how important it is to think before we make important decisions.

Joe Wittmer, Ph.D. and Diane W. Thompson, M.Ed.

SECTION V
PERSONAL ASSESSMENT AND AWARENESS

Personal and academic growth are closely related to our striving to understand ourselves better. That is, the better we know and understand ourselves, the more open we are to personal and academic improvement. In addition, the ability to assess our impact on those around us, and on our overall environment, also coincides with our personal and academic growth. Unfortunately, too many of us equate self-search or self-awareness with a kind of amateur psychoanalytic process where we attempt to interpret own behaviors and explain why we do the things we do. Self-assessment is taking inventory of ourselves. It is an honest and open examination of thoughts, feelings, values, significant events, and influencing factors in our lives. It should be acknowledged that "facing the truth about ourselves" is almost always positive. However, it will often bring about psychological pain in the process. That is, as we learn more about the "negative" aspects of ourselves, some personal, psychological pain is sure to follow.

In a sense, self-assessment involves taking stock of ourself and saying honestly, "This is who I am," or "This is what I tend to be like, and this is how others tend to see me." Or, "This is what I am becoming and this is what I would like to be." As a consequence of this thinking process, we can gain more insight, take more responsibility, set goals, and do what it takes to accomplish our goals.

Self-assessment is often thought to be a common part of our everyday life. That is, we think about ourselves throughout the day, mentally talking with ourselves. Sometimes we chastise, and sometimes we praise. Many times, we apply labels to ourselves, based on the value system that we have within ourselves and the conclusions we have reached based on what we have accomplished. (We are smart or stupid; strong or weak; good or bad; effective or incompetent.) Such value judgments, without exploration of our behaviors and the consequences of those behaviors, can be self-defeating. Too often such judgments obscure personal insights, which can be gained by avoiding general labels and focusing on feelings and behaviors that are involved in the experience. Getting a perspective on life is not easy without a systematic self-assessment of ourselves and the problems that we encounter on a day to day basis.

Self-assessment is somewhat like talking to ourselves about ourselves. However, when we do this our personal defenses come into play and may distort or deny valuable information. Therefore, it can be helpful to involve others in the process and encourage them to provide us with some feedback on our behaviors (the impact we have on others). They can tell us the kind of impact that our behavior is having on them. They need not judge us as good or bad or as right or wrong—although some cannot resist. Rather, their impressions of what they experience when we behave in a certain manner is the most valuable part.

Some individuals are simply too severe on themselves. Others have mistakenly appraised themselves in one way, only to be confronted by others who see them in a different light. Between a private self-appraisal and a public self-appraisal, that is, in the presence of a group of people, there is an opportunity for persons to learn the most about themselves. Thus, in this section we've compiled several large group guidance activities that we think will facilitate self-assessment. A reminder: These activities are only as growth producing as you make them. They will produce self-disclosure. However, using your best facilitative counseling responses with the data they generate is the most important!

Activity 5.1

What Am I Really Like?

Level:	Grades 6 to 112
Purpose:	To provide the students the opportunity to evaluate themselves in terms of 40 different adjectives, to do a self-appraisal on 30 items, and to discuss their responses with others.
Materials:	A "Self-Evaluation Survey" worksheet and a "Self-Appraisal Inventory" for each student. You may choose to use one or both of the assessment instruments.
Activity:	Begin by passing out copies of the worksheet or worksheets to each student. Describe the instrument and discuss how to complete the items. After the students complete the task, place them into small groups, appoint a leader for each group, and ask everyone to share something they have learned about themselves..
Closure:	Return to the larger group and ask each leader to give a brief synopsis of the discussion held in their group. Ask for volunteers to share parts of their evaluation. Close by asking if they would have evaluated themselves a year ago as they did today? How would they evaluate themselves one year from now? The following questions can also be used for discussion:

a. *How did you feel about sharing your self-appraisal items?*

b. *What were the main themes and topics of your inventory results?*

c. *What do these results tell you about yourself?*

d. *How did you feel as you gave and received comments in your small group?*

e. *What were the most important things you learned about yourself and your group members?*

Self-Evaluation Survey

Place an "X" under the category that best "fits" you (for each of the 40 words):

	Very Much Like Me	Like Me	Not Like Me	Very Much Not Like Me			Very Much Like Me	Like Me	Not Like Me	Very Much Not Like Me
1. Active	___	___	___	___	21. Friendly	___	___	___	___
2. Adventurous	___	___	___	___	22. Flirtatious	___	___	___	___
3. Aggressive	___	___	___	___	23. Forceful	___	___	___	___
4. Ambitious	___	___	___	___	24. Generous	___	___	___	___
5. Artistic	___	___	___	___	25. Gentle	___	___	___	___
6. Capable	___	___	___	___	26. Good-natured	___	___	___	___
7. Complicated	___	___	___	___	27. Hard-headed	___	___	___	___
8. Cheerful	___	___	___	___	28. Honest	___	___	___	___
9. Confident	___	___	___	___	29. Humorous	___	___	___	___
10. Conformist	___	___	___	___	30. Idealistic	___	___	___	___
11. Changeable	___	___	___	___	31. Intelligent	___	___	___	___
12. Daring	___	___	___	___	32. Mature	___	___	___	___
13. Deliberate	___	___	___	___	33. Rebellious	___	___	___	___
14. Dependable	___	___	___	___	34. Sensitive	___	___	___	___
15. Clever	___	___	___	___	35. Sarcastic	___	___	___	___
16. Easygoing	___	___	___	___	36. Sociable	___	___	___	___
17. Efficient	___	___	___	___	37. Stubborn	___	___	___	___
18. Enthusiastic	___	___	___	___	38. Superstitious	___	___	___	___
19. Excitable	___	___	___	___	39. Talkative	___	___	___	___
20. Frank	___	___	___	___	40. Witty	___	___	___	___

Joe Wittmer, Ph.D. and Diane W. Thompson, M.Ed.

Self-Appraisal Inventory

Instructions:

For each of the statements below check the place on the scale which best describes your appraisal of self (SA—Strongly Agree, A—Agree, NS—Not Sure, D—Disagree, SD—Strongly Disagree):

	SA	A	NS	D	SD
1. I have the ability to listen to others.					
2. I feel comfortable sharing my ideas with others.					
3. I have some understanding of why I do the things I do.					
4. I am tolerant of others.					
5. I am curious about what others think and feel.					
6. It is easy for me to be accepting of others' behavior.					
7. I trust most people.					
8. I have an ability to influence others.					
9. I get along well with my peers.					
10. I have a clear idea of my goals in life.					
11. I know what I value and believe to be true.					
12. I work well alone when I need to.					
13. I can keep a secret.					
14. I am able to assume responsibilities and follow through.					
15. I enjoy solving problems.					
16. I can accept criticism from others.					
17. I care about my appearance.					
18. I am curious about what others think of me.					
19. I am a leader.					
20. I am optimistic about my future.					
21. I relate well with adults.					
22. I am happy with my appearance.					
23. Physical fitness is important to me.					
24. I believe we can have a drug-free school and society.					
25. I think cultural differences are to be valued.					
26. What I think, feel, and do can make a positive difference.					
27. I am not afraid to take a stand about what I believe.					
28. It is important to listen to others to share their ideas.					
29. Students can learn to listen to adults as well as students.					
30. I like myself.					

Activity 5.2

I Like Me

Level:	Grades 1 to 8
Purpose:	To build self-esteem by encouraging students to choose positive (descriptive) adjectives pertaining to themselves.
Materials:	"Bingo Board" handouts for each student.
Activity:	Begin with a discussion on the importance of liking yourself. Emphasize that it is difficult to like others if you don't like yourself. You might ask if they like what they see when they look in a mirror.

Next, play "Myself" Bingo: Begin by having the class come up with at least 25 positive adjectives which describe a person, i.e., loving, friendly, smart, kind, caring, fun, helpful, and so forth. List these on the chalkboard board for all to see as well as on a separate piece of construction paper.

After the class has come up with the 25 words, have the students each choose 16 of the words that describe themselves write one in each square of their Bingo Boards. They must select 16 different words. Then, cut up all the words listed on the construction paper and put them into a "hat."

Next, draw the words out of the hat one at time and have the participants mark (place an X) the words on their "board" as you call them out. As someone scores a Bingo (4 across, down or diagonally), have that person share the descriptive words about himself or herself with the class. Keep playing until everyone has shared four self-descriptors.

Closure:	Do a go-around asking everyone to share the one positive descriptive word that best describes them.

Joe Wittmer, Ph.D. and Diane W. Thompson, M.Ed.

Bingo Board

Activity 5.3

IALAC/ADNP

(I am Lovable and Capable/and Don't Need Put-Downs)

Level: Grades 3 to 9

Purpose: To help students understand how positive and negative actions can affect their self-pictures and attitudes and to identify ways in which students can be more positive with others.

Materials:

Activity I: The "IALAC" story and a paper sign (IALAC/ADNP).

Activity II: Five magazine pictures of a person's complete figure or head. Paper and pencil.

Activity III: A 3 x 5 card for each student, colored pencils or markers, masking tape.

Activity I: First, make a paper sign with the letters IALAC/ADNP (pronounced I-ah-lack/ad-nip) in bold print. Hold or pin it to your chest so that it can be easily seen by the class. Move the class into groups of 4 or 5 students each.

Then say: *All people carry an invisible IALAC/ADNP sign around with them, no matter where they go. IALAC stands for "I am lovable and capable" while ADNP stands for "And I don't need put-downs." This stands for how others often interact with us or us with them. If somebody is nasty or mean to us, teases or makes fun of us, calls us names, or puts us down in some way, then a piece of our IALAC/ADNP sign—our self-concept—is torn away.* (Illustrate this by tearing away a small corner piece of the sign.)

I am going to tell you a story to illustrate how this can happen in everyday life. Read the IALAC story. The name can be changed and the story modified if desired. As you tell the story, It is effective to tear off pieces of the IALAC/ADNP sign after each put-down.

Following the story, some discussion questions might be: *How does an IALAC/ADNP sign get destroyed? How do you think people feel when their IALAC/ADNP sign is torn up? What are some things that happen in school to destroy IALAC/ADNP signs? Is it possible to rebuild or build-up others IALAC/ADNP signs once destroyed?*

Have the students share times (no personal names) in school when they felt put down or rejected and their IALAC/ADNP sign was "torn" by someone.

Activity II:

Give each student one index card and a colored pencil or marker. Each then makes an IALAC/ADNP sign.

You might say: *On the back of the sign, write several things that make you feel better when you are hurting because your sign has been ripped, i.e., my friend smiles understandingly, my friend gives me sympathy, my friend doesn't laugh at me, my teacher shows concern, and so forth.* Have several students share one thing that they wrote on the back of their signs.

Then, you might say: *We all know how peoples' "IALAC/ADNP" signs get ripped. Try to avoid ripping anyone's sign. Look for opportunities to put pieces back on ripped signs. Other's signs get ripped by painful put downs.*

Activity III:

Give each team a magazine picture of a person. Tear the picture into little pieces, enough for one piece for each person. The members individually write at least two suggestions to help "put back together" a student—ways to help one feel better after having one's sign ripped. Have the individual students read their suggestions to the entire group. After all students have read their statements, have the group put the pieces of the torn picture together with scotch tape. Have the students write their ideas on 3 x 5 cards and post them on the bulletin board with the picture puzzle.

Next, conduct a brief review of ways to build up people who have been hurt and the feelings students have when built up and/or put down.

Closure:

You might bring closure to the three activities by saying: *Although we all begin life being positive about ourselves and others, sometimes people are negative toward us and tear us down. There are, happily, some ways we can be built back up again. And, if we see someone's 'sign' being ripped, we can help 'put their sign' back together by showing concern, empathy, and so forth. Put your sign on with masking tape and wear it around school today. When you experience a personal "put-down," rip a piece off of your sign. And, if you see someone else being "ripped," say something to that person that will built him or her up. Tomorrow bring back what's left of your sign to this class.* (Ask the teacher to follow-up.) *Good Luck!*

The ILAC Story

Danny was sleeping soundly when suddenly he was awakened by his brother pounding on his blanket and shaking him. "Danny, you lazy jerk, get out of bed and get downstairs before Dad has to come up here." (Rip!) Danny gets out of bed, rubs his eyes, and gets dressed. His mother sees him and tells him to go back and get another shirt. It's all wrinkled and has a tear. "You just don't care how you look, do you?" (Rip!) When he goes to brush his teeth, his older sister has locked the bathroom door. He asks how much longer she is going to be and she yells back, "Drop dead, Danny, who do you think you are... the King around here?" (Rip!) He goes to breakfast, but there is no toast and very little milk left to put on his cereal. Everyone else has left the table (Rip!) As he leaves for school, his mother calls out to him, "Danny, you've forgotten your lunch again. I don't know what I'm going to do with you." (Rip!) "You'd forget your head if it weren't tied on!" (Rip!) As he gets to the corner, he sees his bus pull away. He has to walk to school and is late. He has to get a pass from the office where he gets a lecture about not being responsible enough. (Rip!) He walks into class late and remembers he forgot to do his homework. He thinks, "Oh, well, she doesn't expect me to hand it in anyway." (Rip!) "She doesn't like me and didn't want me to be in her class in the first place." (Rip!) His teacher asks him to stay in at recess to finish his work while the others go outside to play baseball. (Rip!) He rushes through his lesson and hurries outside, but they have already chosen sides. He stands around for awhile and nobody seems to notice. (Rip!) Then, the P.E. teacher tells him to join a team. One of the boys yells, "Hey, Danny, join their team; we got stuck with you last time." (Rip!) Later that day Danny gets his homework back and it has a low grade on it. The teacher puts a sad face on the paper and writes, "Danny your work is too sloppy and careless." (Rip!) When he gets home, he learns that he will not get the dog he wanted for his birthday. "You're just not responsible enough to take care of a dog, Danny! There is no way you can have a dog as long as you act the way you do around here!" (Rip!) Later that night Danny goes to bed. He gets tears in his eyes and thinks, "Nobody likes me. I might as well give up!" (Rip!) Yet, he secretly hopes that when he gets up and puts his sign on again that things will be better. Will it? How long will he keep putting his sign on each morning before finally giving up?

Activity 5.4

Positive Appraisal

Level:	Grades 5 to 12
Purpose:	To appraise the positive aspects of ourselves and to hear positive feedback from others regarding ourselves.
Material:	Paper and pencil
Activity:	Lead a discussion concerning the difficulty of describing ourselves to others in a positive manner. You might say something similar to this: *We often describe ourselves negatively, putting ourselves down. We have learned to be modest and may even resist describing ourselves in a positive manner, for fear that others might think that we are being conceited or self-centered. We tend to think it is okay to compliment someone else, but can feel rather foolish when we compliment ourselves. Both skills are valuable in our personal growth and development. During this activity we are going to talk about our strengths (strengths only—no negatives!) to other members of the group with the understanding that no one will put us down. It will be an opportunity for you to think aloud about what you like about yourself.*

Next, divide the class into small groups consisting of 5 to 6 members each.

Ask every member in each group to write down at least two positive statements about themselves.

Then, the members take turns telling their positive strengths to the group.

After an individual finishes talking, the group members give that person feedback as to where they agree and where they think the individual missed some strengths. No negative comments are permitted during this activity.

Closure:	In the large group lead a closing discussion on how difficult it is for us to be positive about ourselves, but that sometimes it is important to do so. Ask for volunteers to share something they learned about themselves and how it felt to receive positive feedback.

Activity 5.5

Are You a Cadillac or a Volkswagen?

Level:	Grade 6 to 10
Purpose:	To give students the opportunity to conduct a personal self-assessment by answering "either-or" questions.
Materials:	Copies of "This or That" Worksheet for each student.
Activity:	Begin by asking an either-or question, such as: *Which do you identify with more, a Volkswagen or a Cadillac?* By pointing or by actually posting the choice words in two corners of the room, indicate that those who identify more with Volkswagens are to go to that corner and those who identify more with Cadillacs are to go to the other. Each student then finds a partner in the corner he or she has chosen and discusses with the partner the reasons for this choice. Discussion should be limited to two minutes. Next, have everyone return to the center of the room and give another either-or forced choice. The students again choose between the two alternatives by moving to the appropriate side of the room.
	This may be repeated with five or six questions. The students should be instructed to find a new partner each time.
	Next, pass out the worksheets, allow time for completing, and ask the students to select yet another new partner with whom they will discuss their responses.
Closure:	Bring the groups back together and discuss how they felt when they were forced to make a choice. *Were they influenced by others choices? Did they hesitate until others chose?* Close by asking for volunteers to share an item or two from their respective worksheets.

Am I This or That?

Are you (circle the appropriate word in bold in each item):

1. More like a **teacher** or a **student**?
2. More **yes** or **no**?
3. More **here** or **there**?
4. More **political** or **apolitical**?
5. More **religious** or **irreligious**?
6. More like the **country** or the **city**?
7. More like the **present** or the **future**?
8. More of a **leader** or a **follower**?
9. More **physical** or **mental**?
10. More of an **arguer** or an **agree-er**?
11. More **intuitive** or **rational**?
12. More **establishment** or **anti-establishment**?
13. More like a **tortoise** or a **hare**?
14. More likely to **walk on thin ice** or to **tiptoe through the tulips**?
15. More like patent **leather** or **suede**?
16. More like a **paddle** or a **ping pong ball**?
17. More like a **word processor** or a **quill pen**?
18. More like a **falling star** or a **beacon light on a mountain**?
19. More like a **rock band** or a **baroque string quartet**?
20. More like a **clothes line** or a **kite string**?
21. More like a **"No Trespassing"** sign or a **"Public Fishing"** sign?
22. More like a **fly swatter** or **fly paper**?
23. More like **rollerblades** or a **pogo stick**?
24. More like a **file cabinet** or a **liquor chest**?
25. More like a **motorcycle** or **tandem bicycle**?
26. More like a **gourmet** or a **MacDonald's fan**?
27. More like a **bubbling brook** or a **placid lake**?
28. More like a **screened porch** or a **picture window**?
29. More like a **mountain or a valley**?
30. More like **"A Stitch in Time"** or **"Better Late Than Never?"**

Activity 5.6

First Impressions: Should They Count?

Level:	Grades 5 to 9
Purpose:	For students to realize that first impressions given others may sometimes be more important than other times
Materials:	"Should First Impressions Count?" worksheet for each student.
Activity:	Begin by asking the students to think about how it must feel to be rejected for a job because of *first impressions* which one cannot control or which are unfair. How would it feel to know that you were not considered for a specific job because:

"He's too fat."   "He's too short."

"She's too young."   "She's blind."

"You can't teach from a wheelchair."   "He's too old."

"He has a bad case of acne."   "She's a hippy."

"She has a physical deformity."   "She's certainly not very pretty."

You might say: *Try to put yourself in their shoes. Would it feel unfair? Why?* Lead a brief discussion and then pass out the worksheet "Should first Impressions Count?" Then, place the students in small groups, appoint a leader for each group, and have them discuss their responses.

Closure:	Have the group leaders give a brief report on their group's discussion. Then, close by giving examples of first impressions over which we have no control and examples of first impressions over which we do have control. (Use ones that you think should be irrelevant to the job, i.e., length of hair for a bank teller's job.)

Ask: *How are first impressions used to get us to be conforming people rather than non-conforming or thinking people?*

Think about advertising for personal grooming products. Does such advertising help us become conforming or thinking people?

Which would you prefer for yourself and others around you—to be conforming or thinking persons?

Should First Impressions Count?

Let's assume that your school class is holding an election to select a class president. Rank the following "features" in their order of importance (as you see them) in selecting a president:

_____the most popular student

_____the brightest person (highest grades)

_____the best-dressed person

_____the best looking person

_____the most athletic person

Would you win? Why or why not?

Let's assume that you are an employer. Place an "x" next to ten jobs from the following list for which first impressions are, or may be, important.

actor	librarian	Army general
loan shark	babysitter	lumberjack
bag boy	merchant	bank teller
migrant worker	barber	mother
bartender	night clerk	bricklayer
nurse	bus driver	paper boy
car mechanic	pilot	car wash attendant
policeman	cook	preacher
construction flagman	principal of a school	diplomat
professor	doctor	ranch hand
elevator operator	scientist	flower vendor
hair dresser	sewer worker	house painter
secretary	security guard (night watch)	
flight attendant	teacher (elementary school)	
lawyer	golfer (pro)	janitor

In your group discuss why first impressions are important for the jobs you selected.

If you were hiring a road crew flagman, which first impressions might make sense? Which first impressions wouldn't make sense? Check those that apply.

_____ sex   _____ race   _____ strength _____ dress

_____ age   _____ health   _____ hair   _____ cleanliness

If you were hiring a bank teller, what first impressions might make sense? Which would not? Check those that apply.

_____ sex   _____ race   _____ strength _____ dress

_____ age   _____ health   _____ hair   _____ cleanliness

If you were hiring a bag boy/girl at a supermarket, which first impressions make sense? Which would not? Check those that apply.

_____ sex   _____ race   _____ strength _____ dress

_____ age   _____ health   _____ hair   _____ cleanliness

Activity 5.7

I Would Like to Be....

Level:	Grades 5 to 10
Purpose:	To provide students the opportunity to clarify their own values in a personal awareness exercise.
Materials:	Copies of the "More Than Anything, I Would Like to Be.." worksheet for each student.
Activity:	Begin with a discussion of the ways in which people are different, have different opinions, and different values. Then distribute the rank order worksheets. Ask the individual students to read the entire list and think about each characteristic as it applies to them. Next, ask each student to rank each characteristic in order of personal preference, from 1-25. (They may wish to use a pencil since a change of mind during the ranking process is almost certain.) After the students have finished, write each characteristic on the board or have on a transparency. Then take each characteristic individually and write down the number value that each student assigned to that particular characteristic. Add up these values in order to arrive at a total class value. For example, write "Loving" on the board. Ask the students what number they assigned to "Loving" and write that number on the board. "Loving" 1,3,2,2,5,8,6,10,3,3,2,4, = 49.
	Finally, make a list of the class averages in order of lowest total value to highest.
	It should be stressed that the only reason that you want to arrive at a class average is so that the students can realize that everyone has different preferences, and that these differences should be respected. There are no right or wrong answers.
Closure:	Ask for volunteers to share what they learned or relearned by participating in this activity.

Joe Wittmer, Ph.D. and Diane W. Thompson, M.Ed.

More Than Anything, I Would Like to Be....

Read the list of desirable traits/characteristics below. Rank them in order of your personal preference from 1 (high) to 25 (low):

____ Popular (well-liked)

____ Famous (well-known)

____ Ambitious (hard-working, aspiring)

____ Broadminded (open-minded)

____ Capable (competent, effective)

____ Cheerful (lighthearted, joyful)

____ Clean (neat, tidy)

____ Forgiving (willing to pardon others)

____ Courageous (standing up for your beliefs)

____ Helpful (working for the welfare of others)

____ Genuine (authentic, real)

____ Honest (sincere, truthful)

____ Imaginative (daring, creative)

____ Independent (self-reliant)

____ Intellectual (intelligent, reflective)

____ Logical (consistent, rational)

____ Loving (affectionate, tender)

____ Obedient (dutiful, respectful)

____ Polite (courteous, well-mannered)

____ Self-Controlled (restrained, self-disciplined)

____ Wealthy (lots of money)

____ Athletic (quick, agile)

____ Healthy (body and mind)

____ Good dresser (neat, popular clothes)

____ Good looking (cute, pretty, handsome)

Activity 5.8

The Self-Disclosing T-Shirt

Level: Grades 6 to 12

Purpose: The purpose of this activity is to help students to self-disclose about themselves and to help others become better acquainted with them. The structure provides a similar disclosing method for each participant, thus producing a reassuring and identity-building kind of experience.

Materials: A copy of a hand drawn T-Shirt with a square drawn on the front (divided into six equal parts).

Activity: Ask each class member to draw a T-Shirt (or have copies pre-drawn) covering most of a piece of 8 1/2 by 11 inch unlined paper. Each one then draws a large square on the front of the T-shirt divided into six parts, beginning with one vertical line down the middle and two horizontal lines drawn equally apart in the square. As soon as all members have drawn and divided their T-shirt square, lead them through each area by giving the following directions:

a. *In the upper left hand corner of your T-shirt square draw a symbol that you think best depicts this class.* (Members should be given ample time to draw a symbol, but the emphasis is not on their artwork. The symbol only needs to have meaning to them at this point.)

b. *In the upper right hand corner draw a symbol that represents a time when you had an unpleasant experience in school.*

c. *In the left hand middle area draw a symbol depicting a time when you had a pleasant experience in school.*

d. *In the right hand middle area draw a symbol representing something at which you someday would like to be very successful.*

e. *In the lower left hand area draw a symbol that represents something about yourself that you will have to overcome before being successful at anything.*

f. *In the lower right hand corner list three adjectives that you feel the teacher in this class would use to describe you.*

Next, divide the class into small groups. You may use the results in several ways. For example:

1. One member may begin and discuss each symbol in their specific square.

2. One member may discuss an area that can be shared with the other members of the group. Following the discussion, another person shares a particular symbol of one's own choice.

3. In a go-around process, a member may share one symbol and tell about it. Or, that person might share which one was the easiest to think about and the one that was the most difficult to think about.

4. You may ask that all T-shirts be exposed in front of the group and that one member select one that is interesting or appealing and then asks for more information.

Joe Wittmer, Ph.D. and Diane W. Thompson, M.Ed.

5. After each member has shared one or two symbols, a member might be given an opportunity to look around the group and request more information regarding a particular symbol.

It is not necessary that a person be pressed to reveal everything put on the T-shirt. It should be emphasized that the T-shirt could well change within another time period—for example, within one or two days or within the next half hour. Moreover, a person may have decided to select one of several choices to reveal on his or her T-shirt. This may lead to a discussion of why the member selected that symbol to reveal to the group and why others were omitted. Several students have indicated after the experience that they wanted an opportunity to change a symbol. There may be some members who risk something of themselves, yet do not feel comfortable sharing it with the group. In general, it is best for students to volunteer to share what they have drawn.

Closure:

After the initial self-disclosing process, encourage all members to look for common themes that seem to run through the shared symbols. Lead a closing discussion on these themes.

Variations:

The self-disclosing T-shirt is only a vehicle to promote the process of self-disclosure. It should not become an end in itself. The directions for using symbols may be altered for various groups. For example, you might ask students to list in various parts of the T-shirt the following:

- The most embarrassing moment in one's life.

- The most important belief about oneself.

- Something that might be expected to happen to a person within the next five years.

- The most or the least liked experience.

- A favorite or least favorite television program.

- School subjects most and least liked.

- A unique part of oneself that can be a sustaining force throughout life.

Activity 5.9

Wanted Dead or Alive

Level: Grades 1 to 6

Purpose: To develop greater understanding of oneself (i.e., both positive and negative aspects) and to create awareness of how one develops a concept of oneself (i.e., through reactions, responses, and feedback from others).

Materials: A "Wanted" poster handout for each student.

Activity: You might say: *Today we are going to do an activity that will help us learn more about how we view ourselves and how others view us. Imagine that it's 1881 and we're living in the Wild West. You are an outlaw. The sheriff's hanging up a wanted poster for you. It says, "Wanted- Dead or Alive; $50,000 Reward for Robbing the Stagecoach."*

Then, give the students 5 to 10 minutes to fill in the information on their "Wanted" poster and to draw a sketch of themselves. Say: *Do not let anyone see what you write or draw and do not put your name on your paper. After you finish, turn your paper over and I will collect it. Make sure that what you write is "OK" for others to hear since I will be reading some of the papers aloud.*

Collect the papers (randomly) and put them in a stack. Pick one at random and read the information to the class.

Allow three guesses as to who it is and then show the sketch. The person whose poster was picked then repeats the procedure, i.e., comes to the front of the class, picks up another poster, and reads and shows it to the class. You might repeat this five times or more if interest is high. Then, give everyone their papers back.

Closure: Conduct a discussion on the following questions: *Was your description of how you act different from what your teachers, friends, and parents would say about you?* Then you might say: *The reason that your teachers, your friends, and your parents might give different descriptions of how you behave or act is because you, and most other people, act in various ways depending on who you're with and where you might be. But, all these many descriptions are still you in the eyes of other people. Many teachers talk about students to their parents and parents often say: "That doesn't sound like my child! My child acts completely different at home." What do you think causes this difference in perception between parents and their children?*

You might close by saying: *We've talked today about how we would describe ourselves and how others would describe us. We've learned that many people act differently around different people and at different times. One day this week see what would happen to your behavior if you pretended that your parents were sitting in the back of every classroom observing you.*

Joe Wittmer, Ph.D. and Diane W. Thompson, M.Ed.

WANTED DEAD OR ALIVE

(Draw a picture of yourself here)

Physical Description: _____
_____
_____

Personality Description: _____
_____
_____

How Your Teacher(s) Would Describe You: _____
_____
_____

How Your Parents Would Describe You: _____
_____
_____

How Your Friends Describe You: _____
_____
_____

Activity 5.10

The Here and Now

Level: Grades 6 to 12

Purpose: To increase awareness of self in the here and now; to encourage self-disclosure, and to provide personal feedback.

Materials: None.

Activity: Divide the class into small groups of 6 to 7. Then, moving around the circle one at a time, each person talks in a "stream of consciousness," getting into an "awareness" of oneself. Both physical sensations and mental feelings can be reviewed. The following guidelines should be followed:

a. Each "awareness" must be a self-awareness. That is, the student must share something of one's self rather than focusing on someone else.

b. Each awareness must be a "here and now" awareness. For example, "I am aware I am feeling anxious."

c. Each new awareness must be spoken by beginning with the phrase, "I am aware of...." For example, "I am aware I am sitting here." "I am aware I am the focus of attention." "I am aware I should be saying something." "I am aware I am becoming more relaxed."

d. "Owning" or responsibility must be assumed for each awareness through the language used in speaking about it. For example, "I am aware that I am clenching my fist." Or, "I am aware that my fist is clenched." This particular concept is more difficult, but it does emphasize the personal responsibility of awareness and sensation.

e. Sometimes it might be appropriate to say, "I am aware of looking into your eyes; I am aware of my not wanting to tell you what I'm feeling and thinking right now."

f. Censoring is permissible. A group member might say, "I am aware of looking at Fred. I am aware of his blue eyes. I am aware of not wanting to say any more".

g. Members stop when they say, "I am aware of wanting to stop. I am aware of stopping. I am going to stop. I have stopped." The next person then proceeds in a "go-around" procedure.

Closure: Lead a large group discussion on the importance of being able to focus on the here and now. Close by asking what the students learned or relearned about themselves while participating in this activity.

Activity 5.11

The Honoree

Level:	Grades 2 to 8
Purpose:	To build self-esteem and feelings of successfulness through using structured imagination.
Materials:	Blank "Certificates" (one for each student).
Activity:	Begin with a discussion concerning imagery and how powerful it can be in influencing a person. A good example would be how athletes use imagery before a contest to help them be more competitive—they visualize themselves being successful in their specific sport, and so forth. Then, have students close their eyes. Read the following to them:

Imagine you are standing in a dark room. It is peaceful and calming. You feel good, quiet and calm. CLOSE YOUR EYES. You can't see anything.... It's very quiet and relaxing.... You begin to feel around and find a wall.... You continue to feel around and discover a door knob.... Turn the doorknob and open the door.... As you open the door, bright lights almost blind you.... You are on a stage looking out at thousands of people.... There is a man talking on a microphone.... He's talking about you!... He's telling all the good things about you.... Listen to what he is saying (pause).... Now the man at the microphone asks you to come into the middle of the stage TO receive your award.... The audience is cheering WILDLY and calling out your name.... You smile and bow.... You feel very proud... slowly you walk off stage and back into the dark room.... It's very quiet again.... While you're in the dark room, you think about how proud you are of yourself.... When you are ready, slowly open your eyes.

Next, allow several students to share how they feel after the imagery exercise. (Most will say relaxed, pleasant, and so forth. Some will be surprised that they've been chosen for an award.) Then, give each student a blank certificate and have them write down the award for which they were honored—the award they received during their "imaginary trip." Then, collect the awards and present them to each student. ("Ham it up" a little.) Ask the students to applaud enthusiastically after each award is presented to an individual student.

Closure:	End with a review statement on the power of imagery and how it can increase successfulness and build one's self-esteem. Suggest that from now on when they look in the mirror and see themselves that they work at seeing a "successful and confident person."

Certificate of Honor

Is awarded a

Certificate of Honor

for being:

 Joe Wittmer, Ph.D. and Diane W. Thompson, M.Ed.

Activity 5.12

The Gift

Level:	Grades 2 to 12
Purpose:	To build students' self-esteem through positive words and praise from others.
Materials:	"Gift" handout for each participant.
Activity:	Begin with a discussion of gift-giving, focusing on how it feels nice to give as well as receive and that a gift doesn't always have to cost money.

Next, pass out the "Gift" handout to each student and ask them to write their names in the "to" blank.

Explain that each student is going to give every other student a gift of "nice" words. Stress that all words written must be positive. Devise a system where the students pass their gift papers around the room so each person can write on everyone else's paper. Ask the students to write what they like about that person on the "gift" paper. You may need to give sentence starters for younger students such as:

I like the way you_____.

I like your_____.

You are _____.

You are special because _____.

Closure: Allow each student to share with the class what they learned about themselves from this activity (in a go-around).

Gift Package

Joe Wittmer, Ph.D. and Diane W. Thompson, M.Ed.

Activity 5.13

Which Person in this Group....

Level:	Grades 2 to 6
Purpose:	To explore the many ways in which people are similar and different; to meet new people.
Materials:	"Which Person in this Group" handout.
Activity I:	You might say the following to the students: *Fold your hands. Now see which thumb you have on top... the right or the left? How many of you have your right thumb on top? Raise your hands.... How many of you have your left thumb on top? Raise your hands.... Now which is the correct thumb to have on top?* (Laughter) *I imagine you're laughing because you realize it doesn't matter; that in fact, there is no right or wrong way to fold your hands.... That goes for most everything else. There is no "right" or "wrong" way to be in the world, just a way that works for you and does not harm others.* Briefly discuss this concept.

And then continue: *We're not talking about morals and values. We are not saying it is okay to kill someone or to rob a bank. We are talking about personality characteristics such as being outgoing or being shy, talking a lot or being quiet, liking sports or not liking music, and so forth.*

Now, refold your hands so that the other thumb is on top. Don't just move your thumbs, move all your fingers. (Demonstrate.) *How does that feel?* (Yucky, awkward, strange, wrong, uncomfortable.) *Realize that half of the people in this room find that comfortable!* (Laughter) *Remember that. There is no "right" way. There is just whatever works for you!*

Activity II:	Explain to the class that they are going to explore the ways people are different and similar through a group activity. Divide the class into small groups of approximately six students. When the students are in the groups, ask them to choose a group leader and give out the handout "Which Person in This Group" to the leader. Explain that they will have 15 minutes to determine which group member's name belongs in each blank. Tell them that everyone must have their name on the handout at least once. Ask for questions, then let them begin.

At the end of 15 minutes, call time and have the group leaders turn their sheets in to you. Choose a few of the questions on the handout and find out who in the entire class fits the specific question(s) best.

Closure:	Conclude by reiterating that everyone is different and special, and stress the importance of accepting people as they are, even if they are different from us. You might close on a discussion of how our differences make our country more exciting and how boring it would be if we were all the same.

Which person in this group:

1. _____Has the darkest eyes?

2. _____Has the longest name?

3. _____Could hide in the smallest space?

4. _____Has the most clothes on?

5. _____Has the youngest brother or sister?

6. _____Can smile the biggest?

7. _____Can make the scariest face?

8. _____Has the most brothers and sisters?

9. _____Has the fewest brothers and sisters?

10. _____Has the longest legs?

11. _____Can make the silliest face?

12. _____Can whistle the loudest?

13. _____Is wearing the most colors?

14. _____Has the longest hair?

15. _____Has the shortest name?

16. _____Has lived in the most places?

17. _____Has the most pets?

18. _____Can hum the lowest?

19. _____Has the oldest parents?

20. _____Can stand on one foot the longest time without holding on?

Activity 5.14

This is Your Life

Level:	Grades 6 to 12
Purpose:	For students to examine the meaning of their life.
Materials:	"This is Your Life!" handout for each student.
Activity:	You might say: *Have you ever asked yourself, "Why am I here?" or "What is my purpose in life?" Someone once described life as that which happens as we are busy making plans on how to live it! Many human beings down through the ages have asked themselves these questions. Apparently, a lot of people are asking these questions today and coming up with negative answers as indicated by the increase in depression, self-defeating behavior, the suicide rate, and so forth. What is the meaning of your life?*

Next, pass out a "This is Your Life!" handout to everyone. You might say: *You are going to pretend you are 80 years old and a big birthday party is being given just for you. You'll have about five minutes to complete the handout.* After five to seven minutes ask each person to select one of the answers he or she wrote and share it with the rest of the group. Option: Have them share their paper within a small group of 4 or 5 each.

Closure:	In a discussion, play the "devil's advocate" by challenging the students to convince you that there is meaning to life. Argue and probe to see if they are really living by what they believe or just quoting some reasoning they've heard before. You might want to ask what they would say to a person who was considering ending his or her life because "life" had no meaning Suggest they ask their parents what they feel the meaning of life is.

This is Your Life!

Imagine for a brief moment that you are 80 years old, and a "This is Your Life" party has been thrown for you. You are the center of attention. This is your moment of glory. Fill out the following questionnaire with the appropriate answers.

Congratulations!!

1. If you could pick three of your greatest accomplishments to be recognized during this party, which three would you choose?

_____

_____

_____

2. If you could pick three special guests to surprise you at your "This is Your Life Party," which three would you choose?

_____

_____

_____

3. If you could pick one phrase that sums up your Philosophy of Life, which would you choose?

❏ "Go for all the Gusto you can get!"

❏ "Live and let live."

❏ "Eat the elephant one bite at a time."

❏ "Do your own thing."

❏ "Do your own thing (but don't get caught)."

❏ "Do unto others as you would have them do unto you."

❏ "Eat, Drink, and be Merry."

❏ "_____"

4. At the end of your party, they ask you to make a brief one minute speech about what people, events, or things added meaning to your long life. Outline briefly the kinds of things you would tell them in your speech? _____

_____

_____

_____

Activity 5.15

If I Could Be Anything, I'd....

Level:	Grades 4 to 7
Purpose:	This exercise is a way of helping students clarify their thinking about who they are, what they want to be, and what they want to do in life.
Materials:	A copy "If I Could Be..." worksheet for each student.
Activity:	Have the students complete the worksheet, pair them up, and ask them to talk about their written responses to such questions as: "If I could be any animal (bird, insect, flower, food, etc.), I'd be an _____ because...." This done, have them form larger groups (5 to 6 each) to share their choices and reasons for making their choices.
Closure:	Ask each student to select one statement from the worksheet and to illustrate their reason for responding as they did to the larger group.

If I could be...

1. If I could be a bird, I'd be a _____ because....
2. If I could be an insect, I'd be a _____ because....
3. If I could be a flower, I'd be a _____ because....
4. If I could be a tree, I'd be`a _____ because....
5. If I could be a piece of furniture, I'd be a _____ because....
6. If I could be a musical instrument, I'd be a _____ because....
7. If I could be a building, I'd be a _____ because....
8. If I could be a car, I'd be a _____ because....
9. If I could be a street, I'd be_____ because....
10. If I could be a state, I'd be _____ because....
11. If I could be a foreign country, I'd be _____ because....
12. If I could be game, I'd be _____ because....
13. If I could be a record, I'd be_____ because....
14. If I could be a movie, I'd be _____ because....
15. If I could be a TV show, I'd be _____ because....
16. If I could be a food, I'd be _____ because....
17. If I could be a movie star, I'd be _____ because....
18. If I could be any color, I'd be _____ because....
19. If I could be any person, I'd be _____ because....
20. If I could be any animal, I'd be a _____ because....

Activity 5.16

Who Am I?

Level:	Grades 3 to 12
Purpose:	The purpose of this exercise is for students to learn more about the other members of the group or class.
Materials:	Pins, 4 x 6 index cards for each student.
Activity:	Give each student a 4 x 6 index card and say: *Begin by printing your first name in the center of the index card. Write it large enough so other people can read it. In the upper left-hand corner, write or put a symbol for (a) where you were born and (b) a favorite place you would like to visit on a vacation. In the upper right-hand corner, put a symbol or write words which depict something you like to do to have fun. In the lower left-hand corner, write three words that your best friend might use to describe you if you were not present. In the lower right-hand corner, describe one characteristic about the specific culture to which you belong (Anglo, African American, etc) that you value and appreciate. Finally, put another symbol somewhere on your card which tells something you are really looking forward to doing in the future.*

Next, ask the participants to fasten (e.g., with a pin) the "Who I Am" card to the front of their shirts or blouses. Then, ask them to find an individual they do not know very well, preferably of a different culture and gender, someone with whom they can pair up. These two "new friends" should interview one another concerning the data on the cards for 4 or 5 minutes. Next, form a large circle with the pairs standing together. Each pair should in turn step forward and introduce one another to the group/class. You may want to ask the participants to wear their name tags to subsequent sessions until everyone knows everyone else.

Closure:	Ask for volunteers to share something they learned regarding a class member that they would like to know more about.

SECTION VI
RESPONSIBLE BEHAVIOR

Students with high self-esteem generally feel self-motivated and have a clear sense of direction. In addition, students such as these succeed in life because they have in mind specific aims or intentions of what they want to achieve and feel a sense of personal responsibility. Consequently, they are more apt to behave in a responsible manner. That is, they have a heightened sense of self-responsibility. They have taken the time to think about what they want to be and where they want to go. They have personal goals and plans. They can respond easily to the question: "Where do you see yourself in five years?" Moreover, they are able to take the necessary self-responsibility to accomplish their aims and thus become "achievers." This in turn enhances self-esteem which correlates highly with academic and personal success.

Each time a person realizes an intention through self-responsibility, he or she attains success and is energized in the process. When each additional attempt is met with further success, it provides fresh ammunition to aim toward other goals. The individual's self-image as an "achiever" is almost a guaranteed outcome. With additional responsible behavior on the part of the individual, the spiral toward higher self-esteem continues. Past performances and successes emit signals that encourage fresh attempts and risks. And, why not? The risk is worth the gamble because higher self-esteem and more responsible behavior is the outcome.

The student weak in self-responsibility is quite a different scenario. This individual generally moves through life displaying characteristics of low initiative, as well as a lack of motivation. He or she seldom experiences success because there is rarely any attempt to act in a self-responsible manner in or out of school. In extreme cases, this type of individual completely relinquishes a feeling of personal mission or of having influence over his or her life.

Students who have a clear sense of self-responsibility set realistic and achievable goals for themselves. In addition, they will take the risks and necessary steps to realize their goals and are thus bound to be more self-motivated and self-directed in and out of the classroom.

Students who behave responsibly demonstrate the understanding that the environment they are in influences their behavior and they are willing to discuss the policies and procedures regarding appropriate behavior in the school setting. In addition, they demonstrate an understanding that the purpose of school rules is to guide their behavior and they accept this as fact. They also realize if they break a rule, they (themselves, no one else) have "chosen" to act in a non-responsible manner. Responsible students also evaluate the ways they contribute to the educational environment—a type of self-evaluation. That is, they take responsibility for their own behaviors and analyze the consequences of using appropriate/inappropriate behaviors in various environments. Again, they "choose" the responsible route. Such students are also willing to analyze how their behaviors affect others' behaviors, emotions, and decisions. In addition, responsible students can explain how their beliefs affect their attitudes and behaviors and behave so as to demonstrate respect for not only themselves, but for others as well.

Students who behave responsibly are also self-disciplined. They analyze when they do and/or do not control themselves. And further, they analyze the behaviors they exhibit that express recognition of human worth and dignity in relating to others.

In order to successfully achieve in school and life, students have to take full responsibility for themselves—both their internal and external experiences. Individuals of all ages often fall into the trap of blaming other people for how they feel, for how they behave, and for what happens to them. That is, they are distracted by looking for solutions to problems by focusing on supposed external causes. It is much more profitable, however, to look inside ourselves: regardless of who is to blame, we are at least in charge of how we choose to feel. Taking the point of view that we are responsible for our responses to the world gives us much more personal power and a higher sense of self-esteem.

In this section there are several large group guidance activities that focus on assisting students in creating more self-responsibility.

Activity 6.1

Problem Moments: What Would You Do?

Level: Grades 9 to 12

Purpose: To learn how feelings are related to behaviors and to increase responsible decision-making skills in problem situations.

Materials: One copy of each of the six "Problem Moments."

Activity: Divide the class into six small groups and give each group a problem moment. Next, appoint a leader for each group and have each group discuss what they would do in these situations and arrive at a certain way of acting out the solution for the rest of the class. The solution is then role played for the rest of the class.

Closure: Lead the class in a discussion after each group role plays. Avoid rushing in with advice; rather focus on what people are experiencing or feeling, and what those feelings might make a person want to do. What information is missing? Would that make a difference in what might be done to be helpful? How can you help people when they have problems? You might replay some of the endings with changes suggested by the whole class.

Problem Moments

a. Jeff and Veronica are making plans to go to a friend's party together the next night. Jeff told Veronica he would call her at seven o'clock, but by nine o'clock he still had not called. What should she do?

b. Levi and Latonya are at a party. When the party is over, Latonya doesn't want to go home. She wants to go to another party where Levi knows illegal drugs will be used. Levi thinks he is in love with Latonya and wants to make her happy. What should Levi do?

c. Eldon likes Rosanna, but he is very shy and thinks that he is not a good dancer. He worries that it would be too embarrassing if she were to refuse him a date. He looks at the phone. What should he do?

d. Chuck's mother and father are separated. Chuck lives with his mother, who is resentful toward the father and does not want Chuck to visit him. Chuck wants very much to see his father, but he is very loyal to his mother. They talk at the dinner table. What should he say?

e. Tawanda, who has always gone to church with her mother, has gradually lost her faith and has decided that it is hypocritical for her to attend church. Talking it over with her friend, Tawanda says, "Should I attend church anyway and not let my mother know how I feel?"

f. Carlos and his father do not get along. Carlos wants to enlist in the armed forces, just to get away from the family and school. His mother wants him to stay at home and go to a local college. Late one night he is talking the situation over with his friend. If you were that friend, what would you say or do?

Activity 6.2

My Own Behavior Check-Up

Level:	Grades 1 to 5
Materials:	Copies of the "Behavior Checklists" (playground and lunchroom) for each child.
Purpose:	To assist younger students to assess their own behavior on the playground and in the classroom.
Activity:	Begin by leading the class in brainstorming ideas about a behavior problem. Next, distribute copies of the checklist to each student and allow time for each to complete both. Place the children in small groups and go over items and set guidelines for group discussion, i.e., We listen to one another by taking turns sharing, and so forth.
Closure:	Follow up by allowing students to share where they are successful and which items caused problems for them.

Joe Wittmer, Ph.D. and Diane W. Thompson, M.Ed.

Behavior Checklist
On the Playground

Do I...	Always	Sometimes	Never
get along with others?	___	___	___
cooperate with others?	___	___	___
take care of playground equipment?	___	___	___
put up equipment?	___	___	___
use good sportsmanship?	___	___	___
stay on campus?	___	___	___
put trash in cans?	___	___	___
wait my turn in line?	___	___	___
not act like a bully?	___	___	___
stay away from street?	___	___	___
play safely?	___	___	___
follow rules of the game?	___	___	___
not play around bikes?	___	___	___
use sidewalks properly?	___	___	___

OTHER COMMENTS: _____

NAME: _____

DATE: _____

Behavior Checklist
In the Lunchroom

Do I...	Always	Sometimes	Never
stand patiently in line?	___	___	___
quietly wait my turn?	___	___	___
talk quietly with my friends?	___	___	___
listen to the adults in charge?	___	___	___
smile at the lunchroom workers?	___	___	___
say "please" when I should?	___	___	___
say "thank you" when I should?	___	___	___
say "excuse me" when I should?	___	___	___
keep food on my own tray?	___	___	___
chew food with my mouth closed?	___	___	___
keep hands to self?	___	___	___
make others feel like they are lovable and capable?	___	___	___
walk down halls quietly?	___	___	___
help keep area clean?	___	___	___

OTHER COMMENTS: _____

NAME: _____

DATE: _____

Educational Media Corporation®, Box 21311, Minneapolis, MN 55421-0311

A Problem-Solving Model

Level: Grades 5 to 12

Purpose: To provide an opportunity to learn and practice a five-step problem-solving model.

Materials: The "Problem-Solving Model" handout for each participant.

Activity: Pass out copies of the five-step problem-solving model and give an example (role play) of how it can be used with a specific problem:

Problem-Solving Model

1. What is the problem?
2. What specific things have you done to try and solve your problem?
3. What would you like to have happen?
4. What else could you do to make it happen?
5. What is your next step? (Something specific you can do within a week or less.)

Next, divide into triads, with one talker, one observer, and one listener. After one round, roles are changed; and, then again in a third round. Thus, all three people are eventually in all three roles.

The first talker begins by telling of 1) A real problem that he or she is having; or, 2) A real problem that someone else is having and the person is trying to help.

As the talker shares ideas and feelings, the first listener uses open-ended questions (what, how, when or where) to coach the person through a thinking process.

After the five key questions on the model have been posed and the listener has responded, the observer stops the interaction and tells what was seen or heard. Then the first talker fills in the "answers" on his or her sheet that the triad came up with.

Change roles and begin again. Use the same problem-solving model as the new talker picks a topic, and so forth.

Closure: After everyone has had a turn, ask the group to talk about their experiences with the model. In what ways was it helpful to each? Role play a situation, if time permits, or ask for "volunteers" to share the process they've written to help solve their individual problem or situation. Discuss how they might help others work through a problem by using the five-step model.

Joe Wittmer, Ph.D. and Diane W. Thompson, M.Ed.

Responsibility Round-Up

Level: Grades 2 to 4

Purpose: To allow students the opportunity to understand how the job-related responsibilities of others impacts them.

Materials: "Responsibility Round-Up" sheets for each student.

Activity: Discuss community membership and how we all rely on each other to perform community-related tasks. Have students complete the "Responsibility Round-Up" sheets. You may wish to have them complete the sheets in a small group setting.

Closure: Share responses from the group and work at getting a well-rounded view of community workers, the tasks they perform (their everyday responsibilities), and how they impact on others. Close with a discussion on "What if these community workers did not perform their responsibilities well?"

Responsibility Round-Up

A community is made up of workers who share responsibilities. For each of the community workers listed below, describe the effect each of their jobs has on you.

COMMUNITY WORKERS   EFFECT ON ME

Plumbers   _____

Mail Carriers   _____

Electricians   _____

Police Officers   _____

Fire Fighters   _____

Clerks   _____

Repair Persons   _____

Mechanics   _____

Teachers   _____

Factory Workers   _____

Truckers   _____

Bus Drivers   _____

Butchers   _____

Grocers   _____

Sanitation Engineers   _____

Homemakers   _____

Newspaper Reporters   _____

Baby-sitters   _____

Nurses   _____

Physicians   _____

Ambulance Drivers   _____

School Counselors   _____

Others:_____

_____

_____

Activity 6.5
Self-Control I

(First of two activities)

Level: Grades 2 to 8

Purpose: To learn that certain statements and phrases are "cop-outs" and how we use them to place the responsibility for our own actions on others.

Materials: Hand out "Self Control is Up to Me" for each student.

Activity: You might begin by saying: *Most of us have, though we may not be aware of it, key phrases that we use to give responsibility to others for what has actually happened to us; to blame others for our actions; i.e., "It is not my fault"; "It doesn't matter anyway." Can any of you think of one? How can we tell if our statements are cop-out phrases?* (They are not responsible statements, begin with you, etc., blame others.) *Let's take a few examples of cop-out phrases and see if we can change them into responsible statements.*

Next, ask each student to think of three cop-out phrases he or she has used recently. They can refer to the list in the previous activity if they need help. Tell the students to write three of their cop-out phrases on a piece of paper. After each cop-out phrase, the student should rewrite the phrase to reflect a responsible position. You might walk around the classroom and help students who may be having difficulty with this activity.

Take a few minutes to share some of the students' cop-outs and how they changed them to responsible statements.

Then, say: *Using responsible phrases allows you to have control over your life. When you use a cop-out phrase, you give someone or something else control of the situation. Now, on the handout, "Self-control is Up to Me," finish the statements with responsible phrases which keep you in control of the situation.*

Next, have the students share some of their statements. Then begin to talk about how they need to also be responsible for the consequences that occur because of the behavior they choose as self-control. Example: 1) If a student completed number 1 with "...I would hit him in the face," then the person would have to be responsible and face the consequences of going to the dean or school principal and maybe losing a friend. 2) If a student answered number 6 with "...I make an ugly face and pretend like I'm not listening," then the person would have to be responsible and face the consequences of angering the adult who is doing the disciplining and bringing on worse consequences.

Closure: *You might close by stating: What is one thing you learned today?* (Allow several students to answer.) *How can the ideas we discussed today help to bring up your school grades? How can it help the relationships with your friends? Your parents? Choose to use self-control this week and be aware of what your choices are.*

Self-Control is Up to Me

EXAMPLES	CHANGE TO
1. It broke.	1. I broke it. (Things seldom break by themselves, there is no magic in it.)
2. I can't do it.	2. I won't do it. (There is almost nothing you can't do, you just choose not to do it.)
3. It got lost.	3. I lost it. (There is no "it" that lost anything—some person lost it.)
4. I can't get up school mornings.	4. In the past, I haven't chosen to get up on school mornings.
5. I can't take out the garbage.	5. I don't want to take the garbage out now. (Unless you are disabled, your body can in fact, take out the garbage.)

Complete the following statements:

1. When I get angry at my friend, I _____

_____

2. When I am picked on, I _____

_____

3. When I make a mistake on a homework assignment, I _____

_____

4. When I can't have my way, I _____

_____

5. When I'm bored, I _____

_____

6. When I am disciplined, I _____

_____

7. When I am nervous, I _____

_____

8. When I find a school assignment to be difficult, I _____

_____

9. When my parents won't listen to me, I _____

_____

10. When one of my schoolmates is mean to me, I_____

_____

Activity 6.6

Self-Control II

(Second of two activities)

Level:	Grades 2 to 8
Purpose:	To develop awareness that each individual is responsible for her or his own behavior and must face the consequences that arise from such actions. To help students replace their personal behavior that reflects poor self-control with more appropriate behavior.
Materials:	A watch or clock with a second hand. Each one of the six "Self Control Situations" placed in a paper bag (or any container).
Activity I:	Begin with a brief overview of the last session and then say: *Last time we talked about self-control and some cop-out statements we sometimes choose to make. We are going to continue talking about self-control, but today we are going to focus on the consequences of irresponsible behavior. Are you ready to try an experiment? I'm going to time you for one minute to see if you can control yourself. That is, you must sit very still for 60 seconds—one minute—without saying a word, without laughing, without moving at all!*

As part of this experiment, I will be writing down the names of those of you who move, talk or laugh during the next 60 seconds.

Are you ready? Get set. Go! Allow 60 seconds to elapse and ask: *Was it hard for you to control yourselves?* If the majority say no, ask them if they could do the experiment for 15 minutes, 30 minutes, 45 minutes, and so forth until the majority say they could not succeed. Lead a short discussion on the reasons the students found it so hard to control themselves.

Then continue: *Now, for the next part of the experiment, imagine you hear the bells for a fire drill. But, this is not the usual fire drill. At five minutes after nine, the phone in the principal's office rang. A voice told him that there was a bomb somewhere in this building. If anyone moves, laughs, or talks, the bomb might go off. Let's see what happens for the next 60 seconds. I (your counselor) will write the names again of those who move, talk, or laugh. Are you ready? Begin.* (Allow 60 seconds to elapse.) After 60 seconds, say: *There were _____ (insert number) people who either moved, laughed, or talked in the first experiment. There were _____ (insert number) people who either moved, laughed, or talked in the second experiment. Why do you think there was a difference in the number of people on each list? In the first experiment, how did you feel when your name was written down because you did not show good self-control?* (If it doesn't come up in discussion, you might say: *Some of you might have felt embarrassed when your name was written down.*

In the second experiment, what would have happened if there had been a real bomb and you had moved, talked, or laughed?

The purpose of the two experiments was to reveal to you that if you don't use self-control, your behavior might cause you embarrassment or get you into trouble.

Activity II: Place a bag in front of the class that contains the following six situations (written, one each) on a separate folded sheet of paper. Then, have a volunteer pick a situation out of the bag and read it aloud to the class. The student who reads should answer the questions, but then allow other students to voice their opinions on the answer to the specific question.

Keep picking situations out of the bag until there is approximately five minutes left in the class period. Then begin closure.

Closure: You might say: *We have discussed situations that involved lack of self-control and we determined some ways to put self-control back into that specific situation. We have also discussed the consequences that come with the lack of good self-control. Work on your self-control at all times. Try to be aware when you are not in control and then try to do something positive to gain it back.*

Self-Control Situations

Situation A You are sitting in the auditorium. Mrs. Gonzalez is speaking to all of the students. Everyone is very quiet. You are not interested in what she is saying, so you take your pencil and stick the person in front of you on the arm. The person screams.

1. Which behavior showed poor self-control on your part? Be specific.
2. What might happen to you because you showed poor self-control and stuck the person?
3. How can you show better self-control when you are bored?

Situation B Your teacher is giving a science lesson about airplanes. You want to be funny, so you make a paper airplane and throw it when your teacher turns to write on the chalkboard. Just then, the principal, Mrs. Peters, walks in and sees this happen.

1. Which behavior showed poor self-control on your part? Be specific.
2. What might happen to you because you showed poor self-control and threw the paper airplane?

You threw the paper airplane to get attention from the others. That showed poor self-control. Sometimes people do need attention. But how can they get it without doing something that shows poor self-control?

Situation C It's suppertime. Your family is sitting at the table. Your mother tells you to eat your vegetables, which you hate. You get very angry and push the vegetables off your plate onto the floor.

1. Which behavior showed poor self-control on your part? Be specific.
2. What might happen to you because you showed poor self-control and pushed your vegetables off your plate?
3. How can you show better self-control when you don't like what your mother gives you for supper?

Situation D   You are painting in class. Gordon walks by and knocks over your paint on your desk. You then take his paint and spill it on him.

1. Which behavior showed poor self-control on your part? Be specific.

2. What might happen to you because you showed poor self-control and spilled paint on him?

3. How can you show better self-control when somebody messes up or destroys something of yours?

Situation E   You're playing monopoly with your friend. You think it's your turn to go. He says it's his. You get angry and punch him.

1. Which behavior showed poor self-control on your part? Be specific.

2. What might happen to you because you showed poor self-control and hit your friend.

3. What can you do that will show good self-control when you don't agree with someone you're playing with?

Situation F   Your teacher sends you to the office on an errand. When you return to your classroom, someone is sitting in your chair. You tell her it's yours, but she doesn't move. You get angry and pull the chair away, and she falls on the floor.

1. Which behavior showed poor self-control on your part? Be specific.

2. What might happen to you because you showed poor self-control and pulled the chair away from the other person?

3. What can you do that will show good self-control when somebody takes something of yours?

Activity 6.7

Here Comes the Judge

Level: Grades 2 to 5

Purpose: To develop awareness that all people are responsible for their behavior.

Materials: A sign with the word "Judge" on it (for the person who plays the judge to wear), a gavel, and a copy of the three cases for the judge.

Activity: Begin by saying: *Today we are going to turn this classroom into a courtroom. You are going to decide whether three people are guilty* (responsible for what happened) *or not guilty* (not responsible for what happened) *of their "crimes."* Prior to beginning the activity, make two columns on the board—Responsible (Guilty), Not Responsible (Not Guilty), and choose a student to be the judge.

Say: *Forget that you are in a classroom and imagine that this is a courtroom. This is the judge* Give the person chosen as judge the judge's sign, gavel, and the three cases. *You are the jury. Will the judge please read the first case.* After the judge reads the first case, ask the class the following questions.

Is John responsible for the broken window? Discuss.

Are his friends also responsible? Why or why not? Does it matter whether John broke the window accidentally or whether he did it on purpose.

Let's take a vote. How many think John is guilty or responsible?

Raise your hands. Have the judge count the votes and write this number on the chalkboard under the appropriate column.

How many think John is not guilty or not responsible for breaking the window? Raise your hands. Have the judge count the votes and write this number on the chalkboard under the appropriate column.

For those who said that John was responsible for breaking the window, what do you think he should do about it?

What could John do so that he won't break a window again?

Have you ever broken a window or something that belonged to somebody else? What happened? What did you do about it?

Judge, please read case number two. You may wish to have someone else be the judge for this sequence.

After the judge reads the second case, ask the class the following:

Did Gloria do something wrong? Is she guilty or not guilty? Discuss. *Let's take a vote. How many think she is guilty or responsible? Raise your hands.* Have the judge count the votes and write this number on the chalkboard under the appropriate column.

How many think Gloria is not guilty or not responsible? Raise your hands. Have the judge count the votes and write this number on the chalkboard under the appropriate column.

Next, have the judge read case three. *How many think he is not guilty or not responsible?* Have the judge count the votes and write this number on the chalkboard under the appropriate column.

What can Mike do so that Charlie won't get lost again?

Have you ever had something such as happened to Mike happen to you? Tell us about it. What did you do?

Optional Activity:

Instead of stopping after each case and leading a discussion, have the students role play an actual courtroom scenic scene. Select volunteers to play the guilty parties (Gloria, John, Mike), the defense attorney, and the prosecuting attorney. You might want to give the attorneys some ideas of the type of questions to ask.

Closure:

Today this class has heard and voted on three cases. From looking at the chalkboard, we can see that the jury found (insert number) people to be responsible for their behavior. Summarize what happened. Then, close this activity by stating:

Any action that you take in your lifetime you are responsible for it. John, Gloria, and Mike could blame someone else for what they did, but in the end they are still responsible for what they contributed to the problem. If you wanted to, right now you could leave this room and walk around school for the rest of the day, but you are responsible for that action and you will have to pay the consequences—timeout, principal, teacher calls home, and so forth. On a more positive note, you could decide right now that you were going to work harder in school and make all "A's." You make that decision, therefore you are responsible for it and you, not your teachers or parents, have control over what happens with your grades. Any questions or comments about this?

Cases

Case 1:

John is playing ball with a group of his friends and the ball hits and breaks a neighbor's window.

Case 2:

Gloria is sitting in class. Another girl calls her a stupid liar. Gloria gets really mad and punches the girl on the arm. The teacher only sees Gloria hitting the other girl.

Case 3:

Mike's mother is going shopping for an hour and tells him to watch his younger brother, Charlie. Both Mike and Charlie sit down to watch TV. Suddenly, the doorbell rings and four of Mike's friends walk in. They pick up Mike's hat and begin throwing it around while Mike tries to get it back. An hour passes and Mike's mother returns. She looks around and says, "Where is Charlie?" They look around the house. Charlie is nowhere to be found. Mike's mother is very, very angry. She runs out of the house to look for Charlie.

Activity 6.8

The Law and Our Responsibilities

Level: Grades K to 5

Purpose: To help students become more aware of the reasons for the establishment of laws and how they help to maintain order.

Materials: Mural-making supplies (large newsprint), marking pens, and so forth.

Activity: You might begin by saying: *Ordinarily we encounter laws one at a time; often, when we have broken one. Yet, one of the most important things about law is, it seems to touch almost everything we do.* To help the students understand, try a "mind walk" in which you describe a typical journey to the supermarket (or to school). Begin by saying: *I leave the house and get into my car,* and continue. Ask the students to break into the story wherever a specific law comes into play. For example, the law says that the car must be licensed. The first time through the story, the children may not have spotted many laws. You can jog their imaginations by asking a few questions:

   a. *Are there laws about wearing clothes?*

   b. *Is there a law about the type of the gasoline in the car's tank?*

   c. *Are there laws about how you drive the car?*

   d. *Is there a law about how food is prepared before it goes on the market shelves?*

   e. *Are there laws about money used to pay for the food?*

Following the "mind walk," have the students, in groups of five, make a mural that depicts a shopping trip to the supermarket that represents all laws to be observed.

Follow this with an improvised story about a town with no laws. An illustration of some of the community members doing anything they desire could be useful. After taking a walk through this town, open the class for discussion. The following topics can be used to initiate discussion.

   a. city government

   b. zoning

   c. education

   d. streets and highways

   e. sanitation

   f. utilities

Closure: Close by showing how the above "laws" and the order they bring apply to "laws" in the classroom, in the school, on the playground, and so forth.

Activity 6.9

The Rudder

(Adapted from an activity submitted by Ken Echols)

Level: Grades 3 to 7

Purpose: To teach students that direction is needed in one's every day activities if one wants to lead a responsible life.

Materials: Two small plastic boats (one with a rudder and one without) and a container of water approximately two feet square (or an aquarium).

Activity: Discuss with the students their personal goals and the purpose goals play in our lives—that they are similar to a rudder on a boat. Help them understand the need to develop a habit of establishing goals and working to accomplish them.

To emphasize the need for goals and the fact that they do give direction to our lives. Uncover the water container with the floating boats and ask them what they observe. Now, push the rudderless boat across the water. (Notice that it will not go in a straight direction.) Next, push the boat with the rudder. (Notice that it will generally go in a straight direction.) Let different students push the boats so that they get the idea that a boat with a rudder is much easier to "steer" in the direction you want.

Closure: Use the demonstration to compare the rudderless boat to someone with no goals or direction in life. These people tend to flounder around with no apparent direction. The boat with the rudder can be compared to those individuals who set goals and have some direction in their lives. They most likely will accomplish their goals and be successful throughout life. Close with a go-around in which the students give one goal each they have for themselves.

Activity 6.10

My Personal Private Space

(First of three activities)

(Adapted from a large group guidance unit developed by Cindy Campbell, Corkey Smeyak, and Wendy Perkins)

Level: Grades K to 5

Purpose: This is a developmental activity for elementary school counselors' use to increase awareness of sexual and other harassment and to teach coping skills when harassment occurs. It is important that all three activities be completed in order.

Materials: A child-sized doll and a hula hoop for each child. (A nine-foot long piece of clothes line rope for each child can be substituted for the hula hoop.)

Activity: Begin this first session by using role play to bring out sexual stereotyping and gender identity issues. For example, playing house using traditional family roles with boys as fathers who leave to go to work and mothers who keep house; career roles, i.e., female teachers, and nurses; male principals, medical doctors; male/female police officers, working on cars, grilling food outside, traveling alone; boys wearing pink; different clothing styles, and so forth.

Have one hula hoop (or piece of rope, if not available) for each child. Hoops should be the same color and size. Take the class outside and have children lay hoops on the ground. Ask each child to get into a hoop— their hoops. Have each child sit down and feel their space; put a hand in and out. Sing the "Hokey Pokey" song. Give each child a tennis ball and have them roll it around inside the bounds. Invite the children to share about their hoops; what they think, like, and don't like about their individual hoops.

Have the children invite a friend inside their hoop and do mirroring activities. Mirroring activities involve having the children hold their spread out hands vertically in front of them and a few inches away from their partner's hands. Hands don't touch. The leader moves his or her hands and the follower copies. They take turns being leaders. Have children politely ask their friend to leave their hoop. Use lights or a bell to signal returning to one's own hoop.

Closure: Ask the children to share what it was like and how it felt to invite someone in and to then ask them to leave. Did anyone not want someone to come into their space? Anyone have too many people come in? Anyone have no one come in? What was that like? Could you bribe someone to get them to come in? What did you want if you reached into another person's hoop (ownership, love)? What was it like? Close by reviewing personal space, feelings, and so forth. Everybody has their own personal space, a right to maintain that space by keeping others out if the individual so desires.

Activity 6.11

Learning Appropriate Responses To Make People Stop!

(Second of three activities)

Level:	Grades K to 5
Purpose:	To learn appropriate responses if you are harassed.
Materials:	None.
Activity:	Review personal space concept from last session. You might say: *Today we will learn ways to politely ask someone to do something or to have them stop doing something we don't want them to do to us.*

Next, teach some assertive, passive, and aggressive responses:

Passive—slumped shoulders, eyes down, low voice feeling scared, powerless, do nothing.

Aggressive—move toward someone in threatening manner, loud voice, feel angry, scared, hit, take, push, yell, and so forth.

Assertive—stand straight, eye contact, medium voice, no smile, feel confident, calm, ask for what you want; say what you want to happen, i.e., for the activity to stop now! say what you need to say to stand up for yourself!

For example, A child takes a pencil off of someone's desk without asking.

- **Passive response**—say and do nothing. Look away.
- **Aggressive response**—Jump out of your seat and threaten, *You had better give that back or I'll tell!*
- **Assertive response**—Sit up straight, look the person in the eye and say, *Please give me back my pencil, now.*

Next, have the children divide into small groups and practice the assertive response to playing with hair, leaving my space, not touching me, and so forth.

Closure:	Lead a discussion on how it felt to have given the assertive response and have asked politely for what you wanted? What was easy or hard about it? How would it feel to be on the receiving end of "real" assertive responses? Would it change your feelings or behavior toward the person responding to you in that manner? Suggest they practice the assertive responses during the week, perhaps at home.

Activity 6.12

Harassment: What to Do if It Happens to You

(Third of three activities)

Level: Grades K to 5

Materials: None.

Purpose: To learn appropriate behaviors should harassment occur.

Activity: Begin by reviewing personal space (first session) then assertive, passive, and aggressive responses from the previous lesson (second session). Introduce the following vocabulary and definitions:

1. **Harassment**—Verbal or physical: unreasonably interfering, unwelcome, intimidating, hostile, or offensive.

2. **Sexual harassment**—Unwanted and unwelcome sexual advances which interfere with your life. May include notes, bad words, and unwanted touching.

    a. **Quid pro quo and/ or bribery**—If you let me, I'll let you. If you touch mine, I'll touch yours. I'll let you see mine if you let me see yours. If you do it, I'll do it.

    b. **Hostile environment and/or threats**—If you don't let me touch you (give me that quarter, your cookies), I'll beat you up (after school, in the bathroom).

Next, explore feelings with the children: How might someone feel if this is happening to them?

Confusion—Why is this happening to me?

Embarrassment—Ashamed?

Guilt—Did I do something to cause this to happen?

Powerless—There's nothing I can do.

Scared—Won't it ever stop?!

Angry—Use it to be assertive.

Left out—Don't they like me?

Then lead a discussion on "What to Do" if this does happen:

1. Tell the person you don't like it and to please stop. Say it firmly.

2. If it doesn't stop, tell a grown-up, a friend, a teacher, or a counselor.

3. If a friend tells you about something that is happening, be a good listener, and offer to go with them to tell a grown-up.

4. If you see it happening to someone else, ask the person being harassed to walk away with you. Then, tell a grown-up.

Next, ask the children to name the category (quid pro quo or hostile environment) that the following situation fits, tell how it might make you feel, and tell them what to do. Divide class into small groups and give each group a situation to answer or do it as a whole class activity.

Joe Wittmer, Ph.D. and Diane W. Thompson, M.Ed.

Quid Pro Quo: Bribery (both get something).

1. I'll give you my cookies if you'll give me your pudding.
2. I'll give you my marker if you'll let me wear your bracelet.
3. I'll be your friend forever if you'll invite me to your birthday party.
4. I'll let you touch me if you'll let me touch you.
5. I'll show you mine if you'll show me yours.

Hostile Intent: Threats (only one gets something).

1. If you don't give me your cookies, I won't be your friend.
2. If you don't let me wear your bracelet, I'll tell everyone you smell bad.
3. If you don't invite me to your birthday party, I won't be your friend.
4. If you don't let me touch you, I'll tell the teacher you took Jimmy's quarter.
5. If you don't show me yours, I'll tell Mrs. Jones you messed up the bathroom (get you at the bus stop).

Hostile Environment: (One gets hurt and the other gets something.)

1. If you don't give me your cookies, I'll put my jello in your milk.
2. If you don't let me wear your bracelet, I'll break it.
3. If you don't invite me to your birthday, I'll tell everyone not to come.
4. If you don't let me touch you, I'll wait till after school and do it anyway.
5. If you won't be my friend, I'll tell people bad things about you.

Closure: Review the objectives of each of the three sessions and close by stressing that no one likes to be harassed and that such activity, on the part of anyone, should be reported to a grown-up. Also, you should emphasize that: *It is never your fault if you are sexually harassed!*

Activity 6.17

Sexual Harassment

Level: Grades 6 to 8

Purpose: To expose students to scenarios in which they must determine if sexual harassment has occurred, who was effected, and what steps should be taken to correct it.

Materials: Overhead projector, Transparency, Scenario Packets, and copies of your school's sexual harassment policy (if one exists).

Activity: Begin with the students in a large group and review a definition of sexual harassment. First elicit definitions and examples from the class and then show the first paragraph of the transparency. Leave the definition up for reference during the remainder of the session. Remind the students of their homework assignment from the previous session and ask for any feedback on the exercise. Ask the students to continue submitting examples of sexual harassment to you. (Remind them that no personal names should be used.)

Break the class into small groups of 5 to 6 students. Pass out a scenario packet to each group and assign a scenario to each. Have each group choose a reader, recorder, and spokesperson and then read the directions aloud to the class. Call on each group for a summation of the instructions. Allow 10 to 15 minutes for the groups to read their scenarios and answer the questions. If some groups finish quickly, assign them an additional scenario from the packet to complete. While groups are processing their scenarios, circulate, clarify, and encourage.

Next, display the processing questions on the transparency. Call on each group spokesperson to present the group's scenario. Have the whole group vote by raising their hands on whether or not they think the scenario involves sexual harassment. Have the spokespersons give the opinions of their groups. Invite discussion.

Questions for discussion:

1. *How could this situation have been prevented?*
2. *How would you feel if you were the victim?*
3. *What would you do if you were the victim?*
4. *What could you do as a bystander?*
5. *What would be your greatest fear or concern?*

Closure: Review the purpose of the session. Distribute copies of your school sexual harassment policy, if available. Review it briefly and ask the students to discuss it with their parents and peers.

Transparency

Definition of Sexual Harassment

**Any unwelcome sexual advances,
requests for sexual favors,
and other verbal or physical conduct
of a sexual nature....**

(EEOC)

*Strauss, S. and Espeland, P. (1992). *Sexual harassment and teens: A program for positive change*. Minneapolis, MN: Free Spirit Publishing, Inc. Reprinted with permission.

Processing Questions

1. Is this sexual harassment? Yes No
2. What behaviors tell you that it is or is not?
3. Who is the harasser?
4. Who is the victim?
5. What can or should the victim do about this incident?

   Check any that apply.
   - __ Tell a friend.
   - __ Tell a teacher or other school staff member.
   - __ Tell the school counselor.
   - __ Tell the principal.
   - __ Tell a parent or guardian.
   - __ Take legal action (inform a lawyer or police officer).
   - __ Write a letter to the harasser.
   - __ Drop the class.
   - __ Join a support group.
   - __ Follow the school sexual harassment policy and procedure.
   - __ Get someone else to talk to the harasser.
   - __ Other

6. How could this situation been prevented?
7. How would you feel if you were the victim?
8. What would you do if you were the victim?
9. What could you do as a bystander?
10. What would be your greatest fear or concern?

*Strauss, S. and Espeland, P. (1992). *Sexual harassment and teens: A program for positive change*. Minneapolis, MN: Free Spirit Publishing, Inc. Reprinted with permission.

Scenario 1*

Bill and his class were very excited about their field trip to a local swimming pool. The weather has been very hot and the students can't wait to get in the water.

Bill got right in the pool and was having a wonderful time. After a while, he got out of the pool to go to the snack bar. As he was walking around the pool to the snack bar, two of his male friends ran up to him, grabbed his bathing suit and jerked it down around his ankles. Bill felt humiliated.

Scenario 2*

A certain physical education teacher gets very angry if any of his students are late to class. He assigns extra punishment exercises to the students that are tardy. The boys must do push-ups while the girls watch and the girls must do jumping-jacks while the boys watch. The students are upset with this policy.

Scenario 3*

The whole school was excited. The track team was hosting an important district-wide meet. Three of the runners were expected to win their events in record time.

The three runners won their first heats and were going to the locker room to cool down and stretch out. As they were walking to the locker room, the girls passed by some guys from another team. The guys made some sexual comments about how good they looked in shorts.

Scenario 4*

Each year the school hosts a powder puff football tournament between the different homeroom classes. The girls play football and the guys cheer. During one game, the male cheerleaders lead the audience of students, parents, and school staff in a chant about the girls' rear ends.

Scenario 5*

Each day during lunch, one group of guys hangs out in the hallway across from the girls' bathroom. As the girls go in and out of the bathroom, the guys make various comments about how the girls look and frequently rate the girls on a scale from 1-10.

Scenario 6*

A drama teacher offered extra credit to students who brought in videos of award winning movies. Two students brought in a movie with an R-rating that contained some sexually violent and explicit scenes. The class watched the entire movie over the course of several days and discussed the content. One student felt very uncomfortable watching the movie and complained.

Scenario 7*

Each day before and after school and during lunch and passing time some couples kiss and embrace in the hallways. Some students laugh about it and some students ignore it, but some students feel embarrassed.

---

* These 7 scenarios were adapted from, Strauss, S. & Espeland, P. (1992). *Sexual harassment and teens: A program for positive change.* Minneapolis, MN: Free Spirit Publishing, Inc. Reprinted with permission.

Activity 6.14

Letters of Appreciation

Level: Grades 4 to 9

Materials: Stationery, pencils.

Purpose: To give students the opportunity to express (in writing) their appreciation regarding the positive activities of another person with whom they are acquainted.

Activity: Begin with a discussion on what it means to appreciate someone or something and discuss the feelings involved in such appreciation. Then, ask each student to write a letter of appreciation on one of the suggested topics below. The students should use feeling words (give them examples) to express their emotions in the letter.

  a. Think of a specific incident in which you were aided by someone who may be unaware of helping you. Thank this person.

  b. Think of a person who at one time was interested in your life, but has been out of touch with you recently. Write this person and bring him or her up to date.

  c. Think of a teacher who has taken a special interest in you or has meant something to you in this or an earlier year. Bring this teacher up to date on your life.

  d. Think of a person with whom you are in emphatic agreement about something. Write and tell that person how you feel about this.

  e. Think of a person who has worked hard on a specific task. Tell this person that you noticed the effort and thank him or her.

  f. Imagine you and your parents will never see or hear from each other again. Tell them what they have meant to you.

Closure: Pair the students up and request the pairs to share their letters with one another. Then, reassemble the class and ask for volunteers to read one of their letters to the group.

Activity 6.15

What If?

Level:	Grades 1 to 6
Purpose:	To provide students with situations of vandalism to which they have to respond in a rational manner; to learn how to control their temper.
Materials:	Overhead projector and transparency of Questions a thru j.
Activity:	Place the students in groups of 4 or 5 and give each group one of the "What If" situations below:

What if...

    a. Your family got up in the morning and found your porch steps painted bright orange?

    b. The windows of your home were splattered with broken eggs?

    c. The hedge bordering your yard was broken and your mother's flowers were trampled?

    d. Someone put a dead rat in your mailbox?

    e. The sidewalk in front of your house had insults and dirty words written on it?

    f. You found your father's car tires slashed?

Ask each group to discuss their reactions to the above questions by using some of the following. (Have a transparency ready with these questions on it):

                        Joe Wittmer, Ph.D. and Diane W. Thompson, M.Ed.

a. How do you think you would feel if you were involved in any of the above situations?

b. How do you suppose you would act in such situations?

c. What might be some feelings that people may be trying to satisfy by destroying things?

d. What needs might such a person have?

e. How might a person who vandalizes feel about something that belonged to someone else?

f. How do you think that person may feel about himself or herself?

g. When you are very angry with someone, how do you behave?

h. How would destroying someone's property be different from physically hurting that person?

i. How would you feel after you had destroyed something of someone else's?

j. What are some positive ways of "blowing off steam?"

Closure: Have the students share their feelings with the group as a whole. Include experiences of members of the group. Then, introduce the following topic, "A time I wanted to blow up but didn't." As the students share their stories about almost blowing up at brothers, teachers, parents, and others, encourage them to describe how it feels to control their temper. Ask them whether they think little kids can control their tempers as well as older kids. Ask them why they think as they do. Encourage them to discuss what they do when they feel like blowing up, (e.g., *I used to throw rocks at bottles that I lined up on the railroad tracks or smash orange crates with a hammer.*). Close by reminding them that we are each individually responsible for our own behavior—no one can really make us do something unless we really choose to do so.

Activity 6.16

Who is Responsible?

Level:	Grades 1 to 5
Materials:	"Who is Responsible" activity sheet for each student.
Purpose:	To give students an opportunity to assess when they are personally responsible for their behavior.
Activity:	Begin the session with a discussion of responsibility.

Responsibility is something that is learned, and usually adults regulate the amount of responsibility young people have until they learn to regulate themselves. Focus the students' attention on the two types of personal control (external—someone else, and internal—the person himself or herself) by having them complete the "Who is Responsible?" checklist.

Closure: Encourage discussion after the list has been checked. Ask the students the following questions:

- *How do people learn to be responsible for their behavior?*
- *What responsibilities do you have now?*
- *What responsibilities do you think you should have that you don't have?*
- *When will this responsibility change? How? Why?*

Who is Responsible?

Me	Someone Else	
❏	❏	1. For getting me up in the morning?
❏	❏	2. For fixing my breakfast?
❏	❏	3. For picking the clothes I wear?
❏	❏	4. For getting me to school on time?
❏	❏	5. For making sure I allow others to do their work?
❏	❏	6. For doing my homework?
❏	❏	7. For settling arguments that I get into?
❏	❏	8. For me eating the right foods?
❏	❏	9. For me being home on time?
❏	❏	10. For cleaning my room?

Joe Wittmer, Ph.D. and Diane W. Thompson, M.Ed.

Activity 6.17
Who's in Control?

Level:	Grades 1 to 5.
Materials:	Seven copies of the role-play situations (responsibility script) and the three dialogues (cut apart) and copies of the "Taking Responsibility Summary Sheet."
Purpose:	To have students identify responsible and irresponsible statements and to explore whether they use responsible or irresponsible statements in their lives
Activity:	You might begin by saying: *"**Responsible statements** are statements that let the individual student assume the responsibility for his or her actions. They usually contain the word "I." For example: "I lost my homework".... "I made an A on my report." **Not responsible statements** put the blame on others or things. These statements usually contain the words "you," "it," or someone's name. For example: "You made me lose my homework." "It blew away." "John made me quit my job." Recognizing the difference between responsible and not responsible statements is the first step students must take in assuming responsibility for themselves.*

Then you might say: *Today we are going to discuss responsibility. Responsibility is admitting our actions. One way to admit or assume responsibility is to make responsible-type verbal statements. **Responsible statements** are statements that let us "own" whatever we do or say. They usually begin with I. For example: "I was late today." You see, I am admitting I was late and I'm not blaming anyone for it. I am responsible for my being late. **Not responsible statements** put the blame on others for what we say or do. The blame is external to ourselves. Not responsible statements usually start with "You," "It," or someone's name. For example: "You made me late." I am blaming "you" for me being late. Actually, I am responsible for my lateness. Thus, "You made me late," is a not a responsible statement."*

Activity I:	Inform the students that today you are going to focus on responsible and not responsible statements. And, additionally, that you will be doing some role playing and determining the "responsibility" of each character.

Next, select 7 students to conduct the role playing with the "Responsibility" script and conclude with a discussion around the following:

1. *Who is being responsible?* (Students 1 and 3. Neither student has their homework and both are admitting it. Students 4 and 6 are being responsible. Student 4 has his or her homework and is taking responsibility for having it. Student 6 doesn't have his or her homework but is taking responsibility for not having it.)

2. *Who is not being responsible?* (Student 2 is blaming his little brother. She or he could have redone her or his homework. She or he is not taking responsibility for not having the homework assignment in hand. Student 5 is not accepting responsibility for not having his or her homework. Student 5 probably feels bad, not only because she or he doesn't have the homework, but because she or he made up a false excuse.)

3. *Which of the two statements* (student 5 or 6) *would you personally feel better saying if you didn't have your homework? Why?* (Variable answers.)

Activity II: Tell the students that you and a volunteer are going to act out three brief dialogues illustrating "responsibility" and "irresponsibility."

Ask the students to listen carefully to the scene as you read it. Then direct the students to identify the person in each dialogue who is taking responsibility for his or her actions by using a responsible statement.

Discussion:

Who is being responsible in Dialogue 1? Janet is being responsible. Mary is blaming the test for her failure. Janet admits the test will be hard, but she is choosing to succeed by studying.

Dialogue 2? Bill is responsible. Anne blamed her parents for her choice to not feel good unless Mom and Dad were also feeling good.

Dialogue 3? Neither was being responsible. The class was not being responsible for their actions in class and the teacher blamed the students when she said, "You're driving me crazy." She chooses to lose control. If time permits, you may want to discuss both some student and teacher responsibilities that apply in a classroom setting.

Closure: Hand out "Taking Responsibility Summary." Read the summary together and have the students answer the questions at the bottom of the sheets.

Taking Responsibility Summary Sheet

Responsible—I choose my actions and statements and accept the consequences (both good and bad) for them.

1. Responsibility means that I am responsible for my actions and statements.

2. I am making a choice to do or say something.

3. Responsible statements start with "I."

4. If I say or do something, I will accept the good or bad consequences.

Not responsible—I put the blame on others for my actions or statements and say it is not fair for me to have to accept the bad consequences for my actions or statements.

1. Not responsible means that I am not responsible for my actions or statements.

2. I am saying I have no choice. Other people run my life. I have no control over myself.

3. Not responsible statements place blame by using words like you or it.

Which definition fits you? Why?

How can you learn to be responsible for your statements or actions?

Joe Wittmer, Ph.D. and Diane W. Thompson, M.Ed.

Responsibility Scripts

Use seven (7) student volunteers.

TEACHER: "Before we start our next lesson, I need to collect your homework."

ALL 6 STUDENTS
TOGETHER: "Oh, no!"

TEACHER: "Its sounds as if some of you didn't do your homework. Why don't you have it finished?"

STUDENT 1: "I lost it on the bus."

STUDENT 2: "My baby brother threw up on it."

STUDENT 3: "I forgot it."

STUDENT 4: "Here it is. I found mine."

STUDENT 5: "Someone spilled gooey stuff on it."

STUDENT 6: "I don't have it."

TEACHER: "Those of you who do have your homework, please pass it to the front."

DIALOGUE 1: TWO SISTERS

Mary: "There is no way that I can pass my test in English tomorrow. It'll just be too hard. I think I'll stay in the den and watch TV."

Janet: "Not me. I know the test will be hard, but if I spend tonight studying, I might pass it."

DIALOGUE 2: THE BIG FIGHT

Roderick: "Mother and Dad had a big fight last night. I tried to ignore it. Did you hear it?"

Anne: "Yeah, and Mother and Dad make me feel terrible when they fight with each other."

DIALOGUE 3 THE YELLING TEACHER

Class: All talking at the same time, giggling, and teasing others.

Teacher: (Yelling) "You're driving me crazy."

Activity 6.18

Honesty

Level:	Grades 1 to 5
Purpose:	To reinforce the idea that "honesty is the best policy."
Materials:	"Honesty Quiz" (a copy for each student).
Activity I:	Allow several students to share a time they had something stolen from them and a time someone lied to them.
Activity II:	Hand out the "Honesty Quiz." Read the Quiz to the students, permit them time to respond with "true" or "false" to each item, then discuss each one, making sure to give them the correct answers.
Activity III:	Play the "Liar's Game" with the class. This is a fun way for the students to remember the importance of being honest.
Directions:	A student comes to the front of the class and shares an event that occurred in his or her life (the truth) or about a fictional event (a lie). Ask the class to determine if the student is lying or telling the truth. (Students love to make up wild events and/or a share a real event that occurred in their lives.)
Closure:	Restate how important it is to be honest in our relationships with others. Also, reiterate how honesty helps us to feel better about ourselves.

Honesty Quiz

T   F   1. Is lying okay for some people?

T   F   2. Is telling the truth important in a friendship?

T   F   3. Does lying help in most situations?

T   F   4. Does lying hurt others?

T   F   5. Does lying help you feel better about yourself?

T   F   6. Does telling the truth help in most situations?

T   F   7. Do you feel good about yourself when you lie?

T   F   8. Does telling the truth usually hurt others?

T   F   9. Does lying never hurt others?

T   F   10. Does telling the truth make you feel good about yourself?